Municipium S( )

A Roman Town in the Central Balkans, Komini near Pljevlja, Montenegro

Miroslava Mirković

BAR International Series 2357
2012

Published in 2016 by
BAR Publishing, Oxford

BAR International Series 2357

Municipium S( )

ISBN 978 1 4073 0943 9

© M Mirković and the Publisher 2012

The author's moral rights under the 1988 UK Copyright,
Designs and Patents Act are hereby expressly asserted.

All rights reserved. No part of this work may be copied, reproduced, stored,
sold, distributed, scanned, saved in any form of digital format or transmitted
in any form digitally, without the written permission of the Publisher.

BAR Publishing is the trading name of British Archaeological Reports (Oxford) Ltd.
British Archaeological Reports was first incorporated in 1974 to publish the BAR
Series, International and British. In 1992 Hadrian Books Ltd became part of the BAR
group. This volume was originally published by Archaeopress in conjunction with
British Archaeological Reports (Oxford) Ltd / Hadrian Books Ltd, the Series principal
publisher, in 2012. This present volume is published by BAR Publishing, 2016.

Printed in England

PUBLISHING

BAR titles are available from:

        BAR Publishing
        122 Banbury Rd, Oxford, OX2 7BP, UK
EMAIL   info@barpublishing.com
PHONE +44 (0)1865 310431
  FAX   +44 (0)1865 316916
        www.barpublishing.com

Contents

Contents i
Preface iv

I. Introductory 1
a) Reports by travelers and explorers about Roman monuments in Pljevlja
   and its environs 1
   Discovery, publication and transmission of the inscriptions 1
b) Archaeological investigations 6

II. Local population: natives and immigrants 9
a) Literary evidence about tribes in the central part oft he Balkan peninsula 9
b) Archaeological arguments 13
c) Onomastic arguments: native names on Roman inscriptions in Komini and Kolovrat
   settlements 17

III. Roman town in the region of Pljevlja, Municipium S 25
a) The name of the municipium in present day Komini 28
b) City administration 30
c) The origin of the Roman city 32
d) City population: Romans citizens, peregrini and foreigners 41

IV. Cemeteries, graves and families in the Roman municipium 52
Prominent families 53
The rest of the citizens with Roman names 58

V. Peculiarities of the nomenclature and kinship system in the region of Pljevlja .. 61
a) Names with two cognomina 61
b) Marriage: natives and Romans 62
c) Lateral Kinship: *Amita* 64

Conclusion 65

Abbreviations 67
Bibliography 69
Addendum: Native names in the surroundings of Pljevlja and Prijepolje
   and in the region of Ivangrad 71
Appendix: photos of the inscriptions from Municipium S. 73
Index 83

List of illustrations

Fig. 1: Lim valley 2

Fig. 2: A.J. Evans 3

Fig. 3: Tumulus at Krajčinoviči near Priboj 13

Fig. 4: Tumulus at Otilovići near Pljevlja 14

Fig. 5: Graves in the city cemeteries at Komini 14

Fig. 6: Urn from the Roman cemeteries at Komini 14

Fig. 7: Grave in the city cemeteries at Komini 15

Figs. 8-10: Urnes from the Roman cemeteries at Komini 16

Figs. 11-12: Portraits on the monuments in the city Cemetery II 23

Figs. 13-17: Portraits on the monuments in the city Cemetery II 24

Fig. 18: Municipium S( ) 25

Fig. 19: Municipium S( ) 26

Fig. 20: Remains of the Roman city on the bank of the Vezičnica stream 26

Fig. 21: Remains of the Roman city on the bank of the Vezičnica stream 27

Fig. 22: Evans, Antiquarian researches, fig. 21 29

Fig. 23: Fragment of the gravestone from Ivangrad 51

Fig. 24: Necropolis I at Komini 52

Fig. 25: Central part of the necropolis II at Komini (reconstructed by Mira Ružić) 53

Fig. 26: Necropolis II at Komini 53

Fig. 27: The funeral monument of Paconia Montana (Is 75, 75a and 75b) 56

Fig 28: Portraits of the male figure on the gravestone
of Paconia Montana (lateral side) 56

Fig. 29: Male portrait on the fragment of the funeral monument found
in the Necropolis II at Komini. 56

Fig. 30: Lion – a part of the funerary monument in the Necropoilis II 56

Fig. 31: Funerary monument of L. Cipius Faustus (Necropolis II) 57

List of maps

M I: Sketch map of parts of Roman Dalmatia (A. Evans, Antiquarian researches) 4
M II: Central Balkans 7
M III: The native peoples of Dalmatia at the time of the Roman conquest
  (J.J. Wilkes) 11

List of tables

Table I 20
Table II 63

Preface

The Roman municipium in Komini near present-day Pljevlja sprang up in the central Balkan area, in the region that was not urbanized and was far from the main communications. The settlement grew in Roman times in the valley through which the small Ćehotina river flows, a tributary of the river Lim. Municipium was situated in a plain enclosed by high mountains, not far from another big Roman settlement in present-day Kolovrat near Prijepolje, in the Lim valley. Although far from the main routes of communication, the city in Komini was not isolated. It was connected with the Adriatic coast and with the road leading along the River Drina to the North and the Sava valley. The Roman city lived, as the findings from the excavated cemeteries prove, not longer than three and a half centuries, from the 1st to the 4th century.

There is no doubt that the settlement was granted municipal status. People holding municipal offices appear in the inscriptions. The name of the Roman municipium at Komini is not transmitted either in inscriptions or in literary evidence. It is believed that the abbreviation S in one inscription (No. **1**) refers to the name of the municipium. Although not proved by any other inscription, I adopted the *Municipium S.* because it is generally accepted as the name of the city in Komini near Pljevlja. It figures also in the title of this book

Excavations in Komini near Pljevlja and in Kolovrat near Prijepolje were conducted by Alexandrina Cermanović-Kuzmanović in 1964-1967, and again in 1970-1977. Two city cemeteries were discovered and nearly 700 graves, many of them with inscribed monuments.

My interest in the history of the Roman municipium near Pljevlja began when I visited the region during the excavations in 1977. Soon after, I published the Roman inscriptions from Prijepolje, fascinated at first by the portraits of the people on the monuments. Many years afterwards, I was invited by colleagues who prepared the publication of all the material left by A. Cermanović-Kuzmanović to write about inscriptions and literary evidence. The inscriptions *in situ* and grave goods give grounds to discuss once again the problem of how the city and its population came into being. My principal aim was to collect, comment and republish all the inscriptions from this place and to try to reconstruct the life of the city from the 1st to 4th century, basing my research on the literary, archaeological and epigraphic evidence.

First of all, I would like to thank Dr. Mira Ružić for her help in selecting the photos of the inscriptions in the material left by the late Aexandrina Cermanović-Kuzmanović and in the documentation of the Archaeological collection at the Faculty of Philosophy in Belgrade, and for the many discussions we used to have during my work on this book. I spent nice days as a guest in her team during the archaeological investigations at Komini in 2009. I am also grateful to Dr. Miroslav Lazić and Dr. Miodrag Sladić from the Archaeological collection who, as prehistoric archaeologists, readily helped me to understand the prehistoric situation of the region. For the preparation of the photos for printing, I am grateful to Nebojša Borić, the photographer at the Archeological Institute in Belgrade. I owe much to my friend Mirka Janković for helping me with English translation.

I. INTRODUCTORY

a) REPORTS BY TRAVELERS AND EXPLORERS ABOUT ROMAN MONUMENTS IN PLJEVLJA[1] AND ITS ENVIRONS

Discovery, publication and transmission of inscriptions

The first testimony about the ancient ruins in Pljevlje and Prijepolje area was a note by Dubrovnik ambassadors who passed through the city on their way to Constantinople in the late 18th century. Their short report, *Giornale del Viaggio a Constantinopoli fatto dagli Ambasciatori della Republica di Ragusa alla Sublime Porta l'anno 1792*[2] is generalised, and containing no precise information about the place or its monuments. They saw numerous Roman ruins, bases of statues, marble pillars and inscriptions; an hour later they came across more, in their words, splendid monuments. The information about inscriptions is reliable: they recorded two inscriptions, one of which mentions *eques Romanus* and the other a decurion in the municipium although all that remains of its name is S. (no. **1, 85**). Both inscriptions are preserved until the present day.

Other travellers who visited Turkish Balkan territories also refer to Pljevlja under its Turkish name Tashlidja. On his way to Epirus, F.C.H. Pouqueville, the newly-appointed consul general with Ali Pasha, the Turkish vizier in Yanina, traveled through Central Balkan and Greek lands, including Peloponnesus and Macedonia. He described the areas, peoples and their customs in his four-volume book *Voyage dans la Grèce, comprenant la description ancienne et moderne de l'Épire, de l'Illyrie grecque, de la Macédoine Cisaxienne, d'une partie de la Triballie, de la Tessalie, de l'Acarnanie, de l'Étolie ancienne et Epictéte, de la Locride Hesperienne, de la Doride, et du Peloponese: avec des considérations sur l'archéologie, la numismatique, les moeurs, les arts,* *l'industrie et la commerce des habitations de ces provinces* (Paris, 1820-1821). Archaeology occupies an important place in his opus. During his long trek, among other places, he made a brief stop in Pljevlja. Walking around, he saw a Latin inscription on a fountain in Pljevlja (which he calls Tasligé) but did not copy it for fear of arousing suspicions, as he says, of the mistrustful populace. After him the French geologist Ami Boué was the second French traveller who passed through the Turkish lands in the Balkans and described the population and the region in his work *La Turquie de Europe* (Paris, 1840). His first visit to the region was in 1836. As he passed through Pljevlja (Tashlidja) he copied two inscriptions, p. 357 *ff.* (no. **1, 65**). The transcription and the interpretation by someone called Herr Hase were not correct.

Systematic collection and recording of Roman inscriptions in Pljevlja began in the 19th century. The first one to visit Pljevlja in order to record the Roman ruins, and first and foremost the inscriptions, was Otto Blau, the Prussian royal consul in Bosnia. Prompted by Th. Mommsen he travelled from Sarajevo to Pljevlja intending to take down Latin inscriptions. His short trip resulted in the first copies of some twenty inscriptions from Pljevlja and the hill Ilijino Brdo and a detailed description of the place as it looked at that time. He went on through Prača and Čajniče following Ruskievitcz's map of 1865 and returned through the Banja monastery, Višegrad and Rogatica. His report carries the date of 29 September 1866. That same year, Mommsen read his report at the Prussian Royal Academy of Sciences in Berlin.[3]

Otto Blau reports about the place and its history, the inscriptions and the places where the monuments were found. According to his description of Tashlidja, the Roman city was at its edge, in the village of Komini, stretching along the both banks of the Ćehotina River in a valley surrounded by mountains. The river pushes its way between two mountains, Korjen and Miljugotino hill. Its

---

[1] The city name of today Pljevlja had various forms in older literature, Plevlje and Pljevlje. Pljevlje is usually used by the local population. The river name also has different forms, Vežišnica, Vezičnica, Vezišnica.

[2] Published in Von Engel, *Geschichte der Fraystaates Ragusa*, Wien, 1807, 312.

[3] *Monatsberichte der königlich preusischen Akademie der Wissenschaften zu Berlin*, aus dem Jahre 1866, Berlin 1867, 838-854.

Fig 1: Lim valley

tributaries are the streams called Vresnica (Vezičnica), Verbica and Skakavac. The source of the last one is near the Monastery of St. Trinity. To the north, it runs by the foothills of Boja Breg and controls the passage between Runica and Bogiševac Hill. The road led to Dubrovnik via Gacko and Trebinje. Blau assumes that Jean Chenau, travelling from Dubrovnik to "silver mountains" (today's Srebrenica), passed through Pljevlja in 1547. Hussein Pasha, Bosnian sandjak bey in the first decade of the 16th century, founded the town of Tashlidja at a place where shepherds kept their herds among ancient ruins. The Roman municipium rose in the same area. Blau's description includes information, albeit generalised, about the Roman ruins and the place where the monuments were found. The information about the origin of the town and the construction of mosques is useful as it tells us about where and how the Roman monuments were built into houses and mosques. The original name of the town was Pljevlja after Pleven in Bulgaria, the birth place of its fonder Hussein Pasha and was then renamed Tashlidja meaning "stone houses". Otto Blau associates this name with the neighbouring Roman ruins. A settlement grew around Hussein Pasha's mosque and in 1857-1860 it became the seat of kaymakam. A Roman altar is built into the mosque's fountain. It was there until the 1960s when it was transferred to the museum. After the kaymakam was abolished, mudir remained in Pljevlja subordinated to Novi Pazar kaymakam. At the time of Blau's visit, the town had 460 Turkish and 250 Christian households and a population of about 7000. There were seven mosques; of them, five were made of stone and two of wood. The eighth was in ruins and served as the gunpowder depot. Roman monuments had been used as material for the mosques and some aristocratic houses.

Otto Blau discovered and copied 20 Roman inscriptions. He saw a number of them built into the town mosques and private houses in Pljevlja. Blau provides the following information: seven monuments were built into the St. Elijah's Church on St. Ilija's Brdo and four in the neighbourhood; four Roman monuments were built into Podstražica mosque in Pljevlja, one in Hussein Pasha's Mosque, one in Musluk Mosque, one in the fountain on the square, two were used by private owners. Five tombstones were also found with deliberately erased inscriptions, alongside fragments of pillars, fragments of capitals and other building material. Mommsen published the copies of the inscriptions sent him by Blau in CIL III 6339-6357. Most of them come from Ilijino Brdo about an hour's walk away south of the city. Tombstones and other monuments were built into the St. Elijah's Church (Sv. Ilija) on the hilltop. According to what Blau learned there, the workers quarrying stone to build the church on the hill's slope came across tombstone every four steps they made. Some seven monuments or fragments were built into the church. O. Blau reports the following: on Ilijino Brdo two tombstones were built into a step in front of the altar; one of them had three and the second one two busts (men and women) on the upper part. The inscriptions were erased. A lion's head was above the entry to the altar area, and a relief (gable with a wreath in the centre) was found above the main entrance to the church. The inscription on a monument built into Mehmed Bey Selmanović's house was also completely erased. There was a lion's head built into the village house of Dervish Bey Selmanović west of Pljevlja. Two stone slabs with ornamentation on the flanks were immured in the foundation of the Podstražica mosque. In the yard of the same mosque was a stele of man's height dug upside down into the ground. Only the word *[m]onum[entum]* was visible in the last line of the whole inscription. The permission of the Turkish administrator was required to dig it out. In the yard of the Serhad Mosque and elsewhere around the town there were scattered big rough stone blocks and they could neither be dug out without the permission of the Turkish administrator. Only one side of these blocks was worked but there were no inscriptions or ornaments on them. Parts of pillars and the like are in the western as well as in the eastern part of the town.[4]

In 1880 Pljevlja was visited by Moritz Hoernes, an Austrian student of prehistory, well-known naturalist and palaeontologist (1852-1917), professor and head of the Metals Department in Vienna. He conducted paleontological and anthropological studies in Bosnia and Herzegovina. His work contributed also significantly to the knowledge of the prehistoric time in the central part of the Balkan Peninsula. In the descriptions of the territory he explored he also mentions Roman monuments. A short report about the ancient ruins in Pljevlja was published in the *Archaeologisch-epigraphische Mitteilungen* IV, 1880, p. 186 *ff*.[5] In this case he perceived as his task the revision of the inscriptions taken down by Blau who had spent only one day in Pljevlja. He stayed there a whole week and with the support of A. von Domaszewsky, Mommsen's associate in the preparation of the third volume of the *Corpus Inscriptionum Latinarum*, he took the imprints of the inscriptions and checked the transcriptions. Before him, Heinrich Müller, Austrian vice-consul in Pljevlja also reported about the ancient ruins in Pljevlja, recorded them and investigated the Pljevlja-Prijepolje road and the ruins in the village of Čadinje near Prijepolje.[6]

Information provided by Arthur John Evans, the noted English archaeologist who spent some time in the Balkans between 1875 and 1881 and occasionally participated indirectly in the turbulent events of the time is of great value and significantly more complete. He reports about the remnants and foundations of buildings, monuments and inscriptions in Pljevlja and its environs. According to him, he intended to supplement and confirm what his predecessors had written down.

Together with his brother Lewis, Arthur Evans started from Zagreb and via the Ottoman province of Bosnia arrived in Dubrovnik. His first trip lasted from August until early September 1875. His journey across the Balkans coincided in time with the Nevesinje Revolt and

Fig. 2: A.J. Evans

dramatic international events in the years that followed. In that complex situation the big powers sided either with the Serb rebels or with the Ottoman Empire, according to their political interests. The situation was not good for foreigners travelling through the area. The English government did not support the rebels because it was against the dismemberment of Turkey and growing influence of other big powers in the Balkans, be it Russia or Austria. Evans' book entitled *Through Bosnia and the Herzegovina on foot during the insurection, August and September 1875 with an historical review of Bosnia and a glimpse at the Croats, Slavonians and the Ancient Republic of Ragusa,* reveals his sympathy towards the Slavic people which rose against the Ottoman Empire. The book drew the attention and protests against the state among the English public because of their state's attitude to the rebels and made Evans' movements in Ottoman Bosnia even more difficult. Under those complex circumstances in which the big powers and Serbia were involved, Evans was arrested by the Austrian authorities in Dubrovnik in the presence of the British consul and banished from the territory. He returned, however, in 1878.[7]

In 1882 Evans submitted two manuscripts for publication. Both were featured in the 48th volume of the journal *Archaeologia* as the first two parts of a series he called *Antiquarian Researches in Illyricum*. The book was a mix of travel notes, sketches and drawings. It is an archaeological overview and at times a political treatise. A large part of the text refers to travels through Illyricum. There are also historical digressions and linguistic

---

[4] P. 190.
[5] M. Hoernes, Römische Alterthümer in Bosnien und der Herzegovina, AEM IV, 1880, 187-196.
[6] See Hoernes, p. 194 f.

[7] J.J. Wilkes, Arthur Evans in the Balkans 1875-81, repr. from Bulletin 13 of the Institute of Archaeology, 1976, 25-56.

M I: Sketch map of parts of Roman Dalmatia (A. Evans, Antiquarian researches)

observations. Evans visited many places along the coast and in the hinterland and recorded monuments he saw.

Evans devotes several pages to the Roman monuments in Pljevlja. According to his report, they were grouped in three places: in the town of Pljevlja, in a valley some two miles further out, commonly known as Old Pljevlja, and on Ilijino Brdo (St. Elias hill), located at the edge of the flatlands south-east of Pljevlja, at about an hour's walk.

In the town these monuments were built into mosques and fountains, some of which were made of Roman blocks. This is also were Dubrovnik ambassadors saw monuments with inscriptions in the 18th century. According to Evans, the Podstražica Mosque includes four inscriptions facing outward while seven monuments in the foundations were illegible. In the yard of the mosque was an altar, already recorded by Hoernes. An altar was built into the Muslik Mosque (CIL III 6339). Facing Hussein Pasha mosque was the altar erected by *T.Aur. Sextilianus dec. mun.* S. (C.III 6343, no. **1**) at a place where it was also seen by Dubrovnik ambassadors in the 18th century.

In Evans's view, the remnants of the old settlement were in the western part of the town, on the left bank of the Ćehotina River, at the other end of the Avdovina Bridge. Evans assumes that that was the site of the municipium. A fountain there was also made of Roman fragments, including an inscription (fig. 11 in his book). About 1.5 mile down, next to the river, fragments of monuments and inscriptions were found in the village of Radosavac, near the confluence of the Ćehotina and the Vezičnica sttreams. This could have been the Roman town in the narrow rolling valley irrigated by the Vežešnica. Fragments and buildings foundations are scattered all over the slopes westward along the stream. Near the hamlet of Vidra is the stream called Babiš potok next to which Hoernes discovered the monument of somebody called *Cambrianus* (no. **47**). The foundations of walls and whole buildings were quite visible. The altar dedicated to Jupiter was built into the house of Bey Selmanović and Hoernes saw it too as well as a tombstone decorated with two busts. In this same area, in Koruga, an entire house was made of Roman blocks and monuments; in its stable was immured a monument with an erased inscription. According to Evans, many monuments were of black and white marble. These ruins extend all the way to the left bank of the Vrežišnica where one also sees the remnants of an evidently Roman fountain with a stone plinth which could have been quarried from a rock above. A large stone altar dedicated by M. Aemilius Antonius to Silvanus (no. **70**) was also found nearby. M. Aemilius Antonius, whilst the duovirus, dedicated another altar to Jupiter Fulgurator, subsequently incorporated in the Ćurkovac Mosque in Pljevlja (no. **3**).

Evans paid particular attention to the Roman ruins on St. Ilija's Brdo in the narrow Vežičnica valley, about a mile and a half south-east of the remains of the Roman town (pp. 33-41). Evans discusses at length the tribe which lived in the territory of the municipium, p. 38 *ff.* endeavouring to prove that the Pirustae territories stretched as far as the Lim River. More recent literature about the province of Dalmatia does not discard this idea.

Evans recorded also a number of monuments around Pljevlja. The Austrian vice-consul Müller had already made a record of a Roman monument without inscription, with a genius holding an extinguished torch in the locality of Rogatac in the Vežešnica valley. In Podpeć, about 1.2 hours down the valley there were more monuments. Evans, however, was unable to get the escort from the Ottoman pasha to visit that village on the slopes of Kolašin and had to rely on local Muslims to get there. Above Potpeć was a Serb monument and below it the ruins of a Serb church torched by the Turks. In its cemetery he found a Roman-Illyrian stone which had served as a tombstone in the Serb cemetery (Fig. 19) Like many monuments on the hill of Sveti Ilija this one was also dedicated to the family's female members, bearing Illyrian names of Aurelia Panto and Aurelia Testo (or perhaps Tito) attesting to the dominance of women in the Illyrian society. On the hill Evans also recorded a Turkish fountain made of Roman blocks. He believed that the village was located along the old road between Pljevlja and Jezero on the Upper Tara. Fragments of the cobbled road exist on the Vezičnica, passing by Podpeć. There are more Roman ruins near Rogatac.

As Evans tells us, two roads, to the east and the southeast led from the municipium in Old Pljevlja. At a place called Odavde, between Pljevlja and Brodarevo on the Lim, a stone without any inscription was found and because of it the Austrian consul Müller believed that the road had once led to Prijepolje. Evans thought that the road directly followed the Pljevlja-Prijepolje direction. At the top of the pass in Cičje Polje he discovered a milestone with a text which by then had largely disappeared. From there the road descends to Prijepolje.

Evans also visited Kolovrat near Prijepolje, identified before him by the Austrian consul Müller as a place where one could see many signs of life in Roman times. His report about the Roman ruins does not contain any detailed description. He indicates that to the left of the Seljašnica stream he saw many fragments of monuments, capitals and bases. According to him, sarcophagi and fragments of tombstones, broken pillars and other fragments lay in heaps. The bases of pillars were supposedly *in situ*. Among the worked stone blocks two had inscriptions: one was a three-line long votive inscription dedicated to the goddess *Dea Virago Delia*, which reminded him of Prudentius's verse; the second one was the famous tombstone inscription of P. Aelius Pladomenus Carvanion. Evans accorded his full attention to the latter: in partly damaged lines, after the name, he recognised *praefectus iure dicundo municipii Aureli S(p)lo(nistarum)*, and further down, he assumed that the lines 3 and 4 read *praefectus civitatium [Melc]m(anorum)*. This reading affected subsequent interpretations of the inscription (no. **1b**). A drawing in his work is the only preserved copy of this important inscription.

Fragments of monuments and buildings could also be seen a mile away along the left bank of the Lim proving that the Roman settlement stretched over a large area. The stones included some fragments with illegible inscriptions.

After the Austrian consul Müller Otto Blau, Hoernes and Evans, Pljevlja was visited by Karl Patsch (Prague 1865 – Vienna 1945), secondary school teacher, curator of the National Museum and founder of the Institute of Balkan Studies in Sarajevo and as of 1920 professor at the University in Vienna. His studies were chiefly devoted to the Roman wars in the Balkans. He wrote a number of studies on the pre-Roman Balkans and the wars the Romans waged along the Danube. Patsch's contribution to the investigation of the Roman ruins in Bosnia and Herzegovina is highly significant. As a curator, he paid various visits to the area, recording inscriptions and other monuments. In his own words, he visited Pljevlja three times trying to find and revise the inscriptions seen by those before him and record other findings. As in the case of his predecessors, his chief purpose was to make record of the inscriptions. Once he went as far as Nefertara to check the inscription on a rock published on the basis of the Austrian consul Theodore Ippen; on another occasion he rode across the Jabuka and Seljani passes to Prijepolje. During the visit, he enjoyed the support of both the Turkish kaymakam and the Austrian officers in the Pljevlja garrison. He published his first report, *Sandžak novopazarski u rimsko doba* (*Novi Pazar Sandžak during the Romans*) in *Glasnik Zemaljskog muzeja Bosne i Hercegovine* 6, 1894, 466-488; it was followed by several reports entitled *Archaologisch-epigraphische Untersuchungen zur Geschichte der romischen Provinz Delmataeen* in *Wissenschaftliche Mitteilungen aus Bosnien und Herzegovina 4*, 1896, 276-296, 8 1902, 115-121 and 12, 117-130.

The report in *Glasnik* of the Museum of Bosnia and Herzegovina (carried also by Wissenschaftliche Mittheilungen aus Bosnien und der Hercegovina, WMBH 4) about things preserved on the ground is short and general; it refers to foundations of settlements which are not described and heaps of building material. Attention is primarily accorded to preserved, notably epigraphic, material. Patsch carefully revised and recorded new inscriptions, mostly with drawings. There are very few photographs. He mentions fragments built into Pljevlja mosques Ćutkovac, Dedaga, Hussein Pasha, Muslik and Serhat, in the fountain in Čaršija, in the house of Mustay Bey Selmanović and Sali Bey Selmanović, Haji Aga Popović, those immured in the orthodox church on Ilijino Brdo, and the altar next to the Babiš stream and the localities of Vidre and Radosavac. In WMBH 8, 1902 Patsch carries over the report of Austrian officers about the discovery of the monuments in Komini. The 1912 report offers a brief historical overview and information about the contemporary Pljevlja, description of the monuments, with photographs or drawings of monuments.

The inscriptions taken down by Blau, Hoernes, Evans and Patsch were included in CIL III. N. Vulić was the last to visit Pljevlja with a view to revising the published inscriptions and taking down these not as yet recorded. *Spomenik* SKA 71 (1931) and 98 (1941-1948) covers all the monuments with inscriptions surviving at the time. The majority is accompanied by photographs, some of which were made by D. Sergejevski. This was the last visit to Pljevlja undertaken to revise the old and collect new inscriptions. Aleksandrina Cermanović-Kuzmanović published a large number of new important inscriptions she discovered during the excavation of necropolises, mostly *in situ* or in the vicinity of graves in Komini and subsequently in Kolovrat. Some of the inscriptions were already published in the first report about the results of the archaeological investigation at the VII Congress of the Archaeologists of Yugoslavia.[8] She published the inscriptions from the tombs I and II and from the graves in their vicinity in Papers dedicated to Marcel Renar;[9] subsequent findings from the 1970s and early 1980s were published in *Starinar* and *Zbornik* Filozofskog fakulteta Beograd (Papers of the Faculty of Philosophy in Belgrade).[10] The published inscriptions were accompanied by good photographs; the text was ascertained by inspection. The archaeological context was omitted as well as a more extensive commentary because she was planning to publish all material at the end of the excavations. Outstanding photographs in her publications still constitute a reliable documentary basis for the reconstruction of inscriptions on some of the monuments which suffered damage in the meantime.[11]

*

b) ARCHAEOLOGICAL INVESTIGATIONS

The Austrian military conducted laic and shortlived excavations at the Roman Necropolis in the village of Komini near Pljevlja in 1899. Patsch, WMBH 8, 1902, 115-119, takes over the report with photographs sent by three Austrian officers, Major-General G. Freiherr von Goumoens, Captain Franz Ivanovič and Leiutenant Wilchelm Faltin to their supperiors in 1899. They noted that the the foundations of the ramparts overgrown with weeds and heaps of rubble indicate the existence of the Roman settlement. Their attention was drawn by the necropolis located at the foot of Bijela Gora (Bijeli Breg today), some 100 paces from the west bank of the Velešnica (Vezičnica) stream on the road to the Babiš Stream on the Pojatić estate. The Austrian officers intervened because of a landslide, which had covered rows of gravesites. The southernmost of the discovered tombs was partly open probably because material had been taken from it; only a corner stone of another one was visible. The officers of the Austrian garrison discovered the third tomb (n. III). The distances between them were small. The officers could not establish how far north the row of tombs stretched because of the thickness of the landslide on that side. The tombs included rooms made of big stone blocks. In rooms II and III the floors were paved with large stone slabs connected by hooks and fixed with lead. Tomb I seems to be the most important and larger than the others. Semipillars over 2 m tall and 0.30 m broad protruding 0.20 m were uncovered suggesting a structure above them. There were few grave objects. In addition to several oxidised bronze coins, there were bones, ash and crude pottery shards. A bronze fibula shaped like a snake biting its own tail was found in the middle tomb. Next to the first tomb was a relief block with three portraits, next to the second one a cipus with an inscription dedicated to *T. Aur. Severus Celsianus* (no. **50**) and next the third the tombstone of *Sextus Aurelius Arg.* (no. **45**). The excavated monuments were taken to the barracks and the material disappeared.[12]

Systematic excavations which lasted several years and produced significant results were begun by Aleksandrina Cermanović-Kuzmanović in 1964. The organisers of the project were the Institute for the Protection of Monuments of Culture of Montenegro, the Museum in Pljevlja and the Faculty of Philosophy in Belgrade. The excavations lasted until 1967 and after a short break in 1968 and 1969, were resumed in 1970-1977. A. Cermanović briefly reported the results first in *Arheološki pregled* 7, 1965, 144-145 and more fully at the Congress of the Archaeologists of Yugoslavia in Herceg Novi in 1966,[13] the symposium *Seoski dani S. Vukosavljevića*, IV 1976,[14] in *Starine Crne Gore* VI, 1979[15] and *Starinar* 31,

---

[8] A. Cermanović-Kuzmanović, Rezultati arheoloških istraživanja na području Municipijuma S...kod Pljevlja – selo Komini, Kongres arheologa Jugoslavije Materijali IV, Herzeg Novi 1966, 77-83.

[9] Neue Funde aus dem Municipium S., Hommages à Marcel Renard III, Collection Latomus vol. 103, 1969, 116-123, tf.XXXIX-XLII and the same in Starinar 18, 1968; Nekoliko novih rimskih natpisa iz Komina, 76-81.

[10] Novi epigrafski spomenici iz Komina I Kolovrata, Starinar 32, 1981, 75-79; Nekoliko neobjavljenih natpisa iz Komina, Zbornik Filozofskog fakulteta u Beogradu XI-1, 1970, 75-81.

[11] S. Loma's corrections in reading some of the inscriptions from Pljevlja and Prijepolje is useless as basing not on the inspection of the monuments but on her drawings from photographs (S. Loma, Domaće stanovništvo municipijuma S. u svetlosti novih epigrafskih svedočanstava, Starinar 53-54, 2003-2004, 35-61).

[12] C. Patsch, WMBH 8, 1902, 115.

[13] Rezultati novih arheoloških istraživanja u jugoistočnom delu rimske provincije Dalmacije, Materijali IV, VII Kongres arheologa Jugoslavije, Herzeg-Novi, 1966, 21-28.

[14] Rezultatai novih arheoloških istraživanja na području Municipijuma S. u selu Komini, Simpozijum "Seoski dani Sretena Vukosavljevića IV. 1976, 93-99.

[15] Rezultati arheoloških istraživanja u selu Komini (Municipium S...), Starine Crne Gore VI, Cetinje, 1979, 93-99.

M II: Central Balkans

1981.[16] She published the chief results of the excavations with nice photographs in *Antike Welt* in 1973 and delivered an extensive lecture about them at the Kolarčev University in 1977.[17] In the same manner, without the analysis of the material, she made a brief overview of the results, *Komini – Municipium S, necropolises*, in the bulletin of the Faculty of Philosophy in 1998. A. Cermanović continued to publish short reports in *Arheoloski pregled*.[18] She started publishing individual tombs and objects found, but she postponed the final report until the end of the archaeological research. Regrettably, she did not live to do it. Few tombs were published integrally with all findings. With D. Srejović and Č. Marković, A. Cermanović-Kuzmanović published

---

[16] Arheološka istraživanja antičkih nekropola u selu Komini kod Pljevalja, Starinar 31, 1989, Beograd 1981, 43-52, s fotografijama karakterističnih oblika pogrebnih urni.

[17] Published as Rimsko-ilirske nekropole u Kominima, Predavanje na Kolarčevom narodnom univerzitetu Beograd 1977.

[18] Arheološki pregled 8, 1966, 115; 9, 1967, 113: 14, 1972, 91-92: 15, 1973, 71; 16, 1974, 89.

11 tombs with their inventory in *Inventaria Archaeologica* 15, 1972, 139-148 in line with the rules of that publication – about the conditions during the excavations, nature of the tombs, description of objects, parallels and dating.

The early excavations in 1964 and 1965 showed that there were two necropolises in Komini; the older one, Necropolis I, was on the Bijeli Breg plateau, and the second, Necropolis II, chronologically younger, covered the slopes of Bijeli Breg and a small valley towards the left bank of the Vezičnica stream. The two necropolises are chronologically simultaneous in part, but the largest number of tombs in both of them are from different periods. Stone monuments with inscriptions marked the tombs in Necropolis II. They are largely missing from Necropolis I which appears to be older.

The first round of excavations revealed the nature and type of material; subsequent digs led to the discovery of more tombs and material, but did not significantly affect the conclusions reached by A. Cermanović-Kuzmanović about the nature and chronology of the necropolises. The tombs in Necropolis I were packed densely, with little space between them and without any discernible order. In Necropolis II the graves and tombs are terraced and follow specific alleys. In 1965, she discovered 60 tombs of incinerated bodies, which she classified as 5 different types, not all of which have been confirmed in later excavations. The present study which is primarily based on the analysis of the epigraphic monuments, should, it would seem, briefly show the results of A. Cermanović-Kuzmanović addressing, *inter alia*, the inscriptions on those monuments.[19]

In her first report A. Cermanović-Kuzmanović restricted the description of Necropolis II on the first terrace in the western alley. It was 9 m wide. The burial belt was 5 m wide and separated from the path by a wall. She singled out several graves and tombs in the investigated area 33 m long. The paper of D. Srejović contributed significantly to the study of the topography of Necropolis II and the link between graves and tombs and individual inscriptions. He also reconstructed two tombs which could be linked to specific individuals mentioned on inscriptions.[20]

On the southern side of the alley two structures (tombs I and II) were found; they were made of large stone blocks and slabs. Tomb I: 3.74 x 3.34 m, 1.50 m tall. On the inside, next to the east wall, was a tomb in the shape of a stone coffin, 150 x 100 x 0.75 m The cipus of A. Maximus Argenianus was found on it. Tomb II, 4.88 x 3.30 x 1.20, was constructed in the same way as tomb I. Inside, along the east wall, there were two stone coffins, one of which was added at a later stage. Cipus of Paconia Montana is over the central coffin and the cipus of Lucius Paconius Barbarus over the tomb added later. These were, evidently, family tombs. Tomb I had been looted earlier while in tomb II there were two oblong stone urns shaped as miniature sarcophagi with a two-slope roof and acroteria. In the added coffin was another urn of the same shape.

Another row of graves continues northward some 8 m away from these tombs. Yet another tomb was discovered there (tomb III). Next to its façade at its south-eastern corner the stele of Aulus Gabinius was found erected by Flavius Aper bf.cos. Right next to it are two pedestals with steles, but there was nothing on them (stele 1 and 2). Five more steles with inscriptions were found in the same row, at the north-eastern corner of tomb III. If they are taken into consideration together with stone urns in tomb I, then 6 tombstones may be associated with them. The charred remains were found in ceramic urns or miniature stone sarcophagi.

A. Cermanović-Kuzmanović dated the burials in Necropolis II to the beginning of the 1st to the first half of the 3rd century. The majority of the inscribed stones belong to the 2nd ant 3rd century. The epigraphic proof she quotes is indirect: the name Aelius is missing from the inscription although one would expect to find it in the case of those who acquired the Roman civil rights under Hadrian, i.e. in the first half of the 2nd century. On the other hand, there are a number of monuments with the gentile name of Aurelius after the emperors from Marcus Aurelius to Caracalla.

A. Cermanović-Kuzmanović wrote several studies on the interpretation of the Komini material. She wrote a short study about the Illyrian element in the archaeological material from the necropolises and about the Roman-Illyrian sculpture and portraits on monuments in Pljevlja and Prijepolje.[21] A wide area of the Central Balkans is now better known due to excavations of the Roman cemeteries in Komini.

---

[19] A detailed overview of all excavated tombs, an analysis of grave objects and a study of both necropolises should be found in the book by Mira Ružić which is in preoaration.

[20] D. Srejović, Grobnice Aurelije Maksimine i Pakonije Montane u Kominima (Municipijum S), Zbornik Narodnog muzeja VIII posvećen Djordju Mano-Zisiju, Beograd 1975, 177 i d.

[21] Vorrömische Elemente in der Kultur des Municipium S. im Dorfe Komini, Živa antika 30, 1980, 227-232; Rimsko-ilirska plastika u Kominima, Živa antika 28, 1978, 325-330; Die Porträts an den Grabdenkmälern aus komini und Kolovrat, Balcanica 23, 1972, 441-446.

II. LOCAL POPULATION: NATIVES AND IMMIGRANTS

As evidenced by a large number of Illyrian and other names on the inscriptions, there was a strong native component in the population of the Roman city in Komini and its vicinity. Its origin could be explained in different ways: It can be assumed that this was the pre-Roman population at Komini near Pljevlja and Kolovar near Prijepolje, that is the native population living there and in a wider Central Balkan region whom the Romans found there; but is is also possible that the majority of them represented the imigrants from other Illyrian lands who had moved in individually or were resettled there as a group by the Romans. One can talk about the non-Roman, native population in the valleys of the Lim and the Ćehotina and their tributaries on the basis of (a) information about the tribes in the Central Balkan region in literary sources, (b) pre-historical archaeological finds from the area of the Lim basin and the material from the Roman cemeteries, Necropois I and II in Komini and (c) last but not least, largely on the basis of the onomastic material in Roman inscriptions on tombstones. The information provided directly or indirectly by these three types of sources does still not suffice to draw reliable conclusions about the pre-Roman population in the area or to determine the origin of those mentioned on the Roman tombstones and other monuments, but it makes possible some hypothesis about it. Literary sources do not provide direct information about the population of Illyricum in areas removed from the coast; the archaeological investigations of the pre-Roman strata have so far been few and limited mainly to the investigation of tumuli which characterise the burials probably until the sixth century BC. The population of the town left visible marks in the material of the necropolises, first and foremost in the onomastics on the Roman inscriptions. However, it is difficult to single out the stratum which could be associated with the native populations of the area at the protohistoric times. A large number of people moved in during the Roman period probably from central Dalmatia where the names belong to the same onomastic group as those on the inscriptions around Pljevlja and Prijepolje.

a) LITERARY EVIDENCE AND TRIBES IN THE CENTRAL PART OF THE BALKAN PENINSULA

Ancient authors, even when they do mention Balkan tribes, do not provide precise information concerning the pre-Roman times. At least information about the ethnic affiliation of individuals or groups are few. In other words, there are no details about the ethnic map of the Central Balkans in pre-Roman times. None of the tribes mentioned by ancient Greek or Roman authors can be reliably associated with the area between the Tara, the Piva and the Lim rivers and that includes the area where large Roman settlements at Komini and Kolovrat were built.

The information left by ancient authors leaves room for various hypotheses but does not permit to determine the location and the territory of individual tribes except for the largest and strongest ones which lived near the sea or in the neighbourhood of Macedonia. The chief difficulty in the investigation is the fact that many tribes in the Central Balkans did not have a clearly defined territory. Even when the border between the tribes did exist, it was unstable and changeable in view of constant movements and migrations. It is difficult to believe that every tribe had its clear boundaries since the majority of these tribes had not attained yet the political organisation capable of controlling the boundaries of their land. Moreover, there were many shifts and migrations caused by hunger or mutual conflict, wars with Macedonian kings and finally with the Romans. The information provided by authors that would permit discussing the area inhabited by a tribe can, therefore, apply only to a period which is also difficult to define. Moreover, the authors did not supply the timeframes so that it is difficult to relate them to a specific historical period. A large number of Illyrian tribes in the central part of the Balkan Peninsula is mentioned by various authors but not one of them can be reliably situated in the area of today's Pljevlja and Prijepolje. One can talk therefore only about where the

Romans found some tribes when they started the conquest of the central part of the Balkans towards the end of the second century. The sources, however, do not always contain precise information even about that. The authors do not say anything about the routes taken by the Roman troops and which area they conquered and instead refer only to the tribes they clashed with and strongholds they besieged. Today it is difficult to establish with certainty the sequence of events and the location of such strongholds. Some authors, e.g. Apian, used official sources such as Octavianus' report to the Senate about the war in Illyricum in 35-33 BC. The report mostly talks about those who offered fierce resistance and thus made it into the report to the Roman Senate as the evidence of the deserved triumph. Strabo describes the land and the people but even he does not provide precise geographical information, particularly regarding the tribes further away from principal routes so that he is not of much help when it comes to identifying the areas where individual tribes lived. He lists the tribes and on the basis of the order in which he does it, it is possible sometimes to gain a picture of their location. Pliny is one of the few authors who provides the census of tribes in the Balkan provinces. He groups the Dalmatian tribes in three large juridical convents (*conventus iuridicus*): Salonitan, Scardonitan and Naronitan. Nonetheless, two things make his lists rather useless when discussing the territory of specific tribes within the province: firstly, he says nothing definite about the boundaries of individual convents so that it is impossible to say how far inland they stretched, and secondly, he does not mention the boundaries between individual tribes. He talks about the size and strength of tribes in the *conventus* and says how many decurias they had. Ptolemy about a century later, speaks again about the *civitates* in the Roman province of Dalmatia This is, however, another period and the Roman organisation which did not always heed former boundaries between tribes. Moreover, for different reasons, the Romans resettled some tribes from their original territories. The Pirustae, for instance, were moved to Dacia to work in the mines at the beginning of the 2nd century.

As a rule, the authors mention the tribes which lived near the sea, such as Liburni, Delmatae and even the Iapudes in the north, Taulantii, Parthini, Dassareti, Pirustae, Docleatae and Narensi in the south. They also know more about those along the borders of Macedonia and Epirus which, having been in contact with ancient states, had created a kind of pre-state organisation and had their rulers and dynasties. The Dardanians, Parthini and Taulantii had an early contact or conflict with the Romans and so the ancient authors are aware of them. Of the tribes whose territory is known, the Dardanians in the south-east, in the subsequent Roman province of Upper Moesia were the nearest to the area of Pljevlja and Prijepolje. They cannot be associated in any way with the area along the Lim or the Upper Drina, either archaeologically or onomastically. It is known that the Dardanians lived in the central part of the Balkan Peninsula and bordered on Macedonia. Their western, eastern and northern borders, that is if they had any,[22] however, are not known, and this holds true also of the neighbouring tribes. The Daesidiates, a powerful tribe which participated in the Dalmatian-Pannonian revolt in 6-9 A.D., is one of the few tribes in the Balkan inlands whose territory is approximately known owing to an inscription from Breza near Sarajevo. The inscription mentions the distance of 146 miles (?) between Salona and the *castella Daesitiata*. The both are nowhere near Pljevlja. The tribes in the south, the Pirustae, Dassareti and others are mentioned in the Roman wars with Macedonia so that one can identify their area approximately,[23] but it does not help to localise other tribes in the central Balkans.

A.J. Evans assumed that the Roman settlements in the present village of Komini near Pljevlja and the one in Kolovrat near Prijepolje arose in the area to which in pre-historical times extended the Pirustae.

The hypothesis about the Pirustae in the Lim valley warrants major attention. They were a big tribe which lived in northern Albania and, it is believed, in northern Montenegro in the Pre-Roman times.[24] In the Roman times part of the tribe was moved to Dacia, to the mining land near the city of Alburnus Maior. Evans simplified the ethnic map of the Central Balkans in the belief that Livy's information about the third Roman-Macedonian War allowed to localise the Pirustae north of the Dassareti who inhabited the area around the Ohrid Lake.[25] Basing his opinion on Strabo, VII 3, who says that the Pirustae were the neighbours of the Dardanians, he looked for them in the Lim valley and established a link between them and the tribes of Maesaei and Daesitiates which he included among the Pannonian tribes. The Drina would be the boundary between the Daesitiati and the Pirustae.

It is difficult to put together the information about the Pirustae in the literary sources and thus define their boundaries. The authors mention the Pirustae in the southern Illyrian area and also as a Pannonian tribe. The earliest reliable information which might indicate that the Pirustae lived also in today's Montenegro relates to the time after the third Macedonian War. They are mentioned in the Skadar psephysm as a Dassareti tribe, *Dassaretiorum Pirustae*, in 165 BC., one of the tribes which were, alongside the Daorsi and Taulantii, exempted from the Roman tax, Livy XLV 26. The link with the Dassareti who lived around the Skadar Lake defines their territory better. They must have also inhabited the area near the Adriatic coast because Caesar came across them in 54 BC when he penetrated the province of Illyricum (Caes. BG V 1,5 ff.) and won it over by diplomatic means.

---

[22] F. Papazoglu, The Central Balkan Tribes in pre-Roman times, Triballi, Autariatae, Dardanians, Scordisci and Moesians, Amsterdam 1978.

[23] On tribes in the Roman province of Dalmatia see Alföldy, Bevölkerung, 32-67; J.J. Wilkes, Dalmatia, 153-177.

[24] Alföldy, Bevölkerung, 57-58; Wilkes, Dalmatia, 155 ff., 172 and passim.

[25] A.J. Evans, Antiquarian Researches in Illyricum, Archaeologia XLIX, 1885, 38 f.

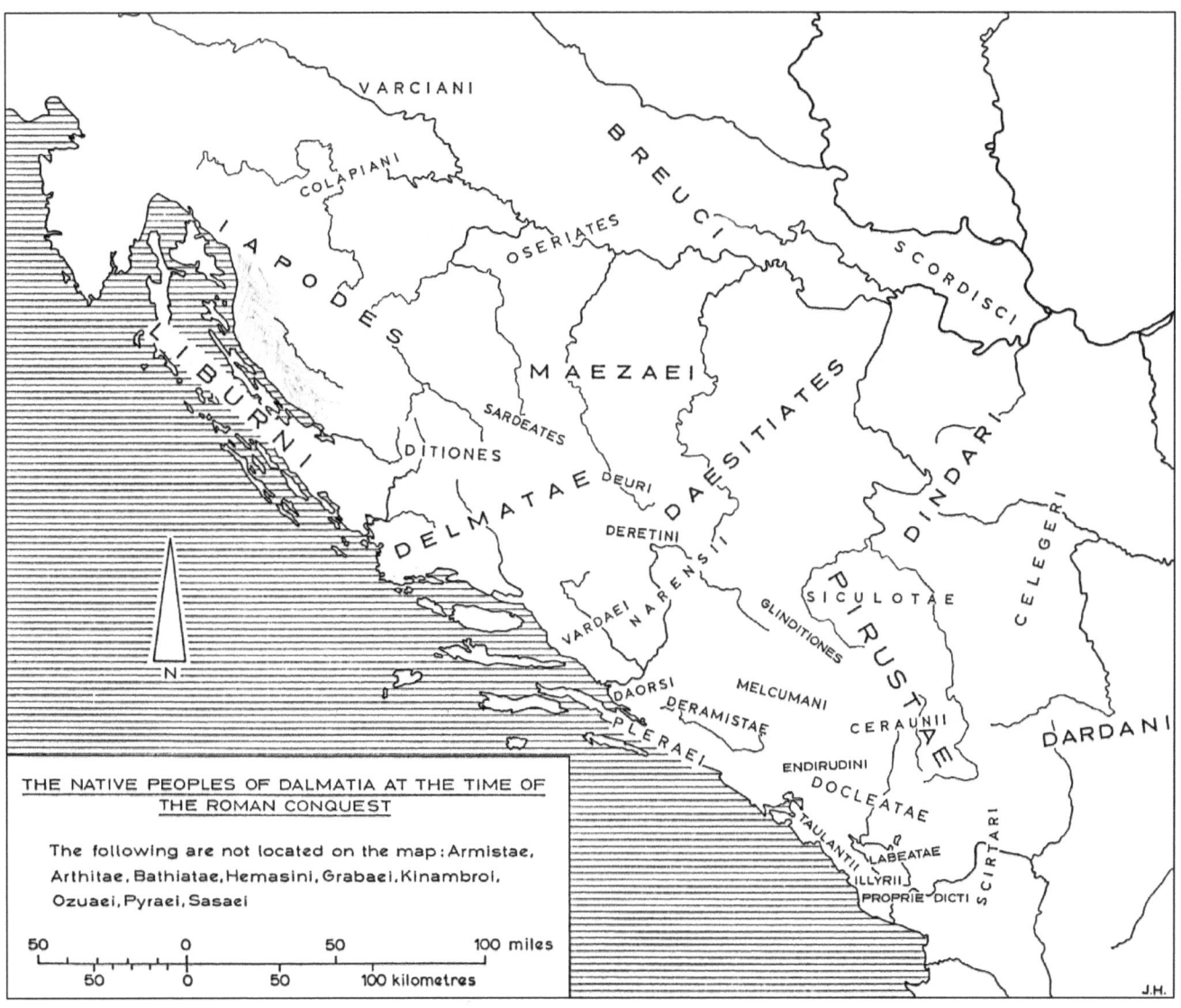

M III: The native peoples of Dalmatia at the time of the Roman conquest (J.J. Wilkes)

They are mentioned also among the tribes against which Octavianus fought in 33 BC. (Appian, Illyr. 16). This information is irrelevant, however, in the discussion about their territory because the tribes Octavianus defeated on that occasion are mentioned according to the extent of resistance to the Romans rather than by their geographical distribution. Strabo and Veleius Paterculus might allow the hypothesis that the Pirustae lived nearer to the Central Balkans area. To Strabo, VII 5,3 the Pirustae are a Pannonian tribe. Veleius Paterculus II 115 mentions them alongside the rebelled tribes in 6-9 A.D. At the end of the revolt in 9 BC. the vanquished retreated with the Daesitiates to inaccessible mountain areas. Pliny does not mention them. Ptolemy refers to them as a tribe in the eastern province of Dalmatia, II 16,5. That they existed as a tribe in the Roman times, is attested to by information on inscriptions in the mining area of Dacia, where they are mentioned.

If the Pirustae lived near the Ohrid Lake and if they were the neighbors of the Dassareti, it is difficult to believe that they could have stretched at that time as far as the area in today's Bosnia inhabited by Pannonian tribes. It is also rather improbable that they participated as the Dassareti neighbors in the Dalmatian-Pannonian revolt. Different pieces of information provided by Roman authors about their neighbors or the information that they were a Pannonian tribe cannot be put together so as to give us a clear picture about the extent of their territory. The fact that in one case they can be found in the Ohrid Lake area and in another among the Pannonian tribes could be explained by the movement of the tribe before the arrival of the Romans and perhaps after the Romans established their authority there.

Pirustae could have lived south of the area covered by the Naronitan convent or east of it, in the hinterland of the province. The latter seems a more attractive hypothesis. It would permit to include the present-day northern Montenegro and the region of Pljevlja in the area inhabited by the Pirustae at some point in time. The hypothesis that they lived on both sides of the Albanian mountains sounds plausible,[26] and can be harmonized with the infor-

---

[26] Cf. G. Zippel, Die römische Herrschaft in Illyrien bis zum Augustus, Leipzig, 1877, 62 f. Polaschek, RE XX, 1920, 1729 ff. G. Alföldy, Bevölkerung, 57 f.; J.J. Wilkes, Dalmatia, 173 ff.

mation about this tribe in the south, in the neighborhood of the Dassareti, but not with this in Strabo calling them a Pannonian tribe. G. Alföldy thinks that Strabo's information permits to assume that their territory spread from the Dindarii to the southern border of the province of Dalmatia. However, other communities have been assumed to live in that territory in the Roman time, among others the Scirtones or Scirtarii whom Ptolemy II 16, 5 mentions as the neighbours of Macedonia. Pliny does not mention Pirustae but instead he lists, in n. h.III 143 the Siculotae with 72 *decuriae* among the tribes in the Naronitan convent. Then there are also the Cerauni whom Alföldy places in the Albanian mountains and the mountains around the upper flows of the Drina and the Lim.

Alföldy also resorts to the hypothesis about these three tribal communities, the Scirtones, Cerauni and Siculotae in the former Pirustae territory to explain the disappearance of the name of the Pirustae from Pliny's list. The Pirustae presumably broke into smaller communities, but not before the Roman time. This should explain the absence of the name of the Pirustae in Pliny's list of the tribes comprised in the Naronitan convents. The name 'Cerauni' could be associated with the mountainous area, perhaps around the upper flows of the Tara and Lim rivers. The Siculotae would be an immigrant people. G. Alföldy situates them in the area of Pljevlja. The names on the Roman monuments around Pljevlja and Prijepolje and the nomenclature formulae might indicate strong onomastic ties with the Delmatae. That is where the Siculotae locality is found. Siculi is the name of the locality between Salona and Tragurium. He believes that the Delmatae from the neighborhood of Salona and the military castra Aequinum and Tilurium were moved away during the imperial period in order to give their land to veterans. The transported Siculotae left their mark in the name of the settlement, *Municipium S[icu]lo(tarum)* in the inscription from Čadinje near Prijepolje (no. **1b**). Further argument for the thesis about the transfer of people from the Salona area Alföldy sees in the fact that the names on the inscriptions in Pljevlja correspond largely with the Dalmatian ones.[27]

The main problem remains however, that Pliny does not mention Pirustae in the Naronitan convents as one would expect if they inhabited the province of Dalmatia, and Ptolemy whose geographical work reflect the situation in the second century, mentions them here. J.J. Wilkes in his well documented book about the Roman province of Dalmatia returns to the issue of the Pirustae.[28] He largely agrees with Alföldy with regard that three *civitates* were organized by the Roman governement out of the Pirustae, these of Scirtones, Cerauni and Siculotae and his location of the latter in the region of Pljevlja in the Ćehotina valley. However, he disagree with his reconstruction of the name of the city in the inscription from Čadinje as *municipium S[icu]lo(tarum,)* proposing as better the reading *municipium S[p]lo(nistarum)*, as Evans has completed it. He is aware of the difficulty how to explain

that Pirustae are not mentioned by Pliny in the 60s of the first century and appear as a tribe in Ptolemy, in the end of the second century. He sees as only solution the possibility that Pirustae were still known collectively as the *civitas Pirustarum* implied by Ptolemy's record of them in Dalmatia, but the expansion of the inscription of the local authority at Čadinje to *[prae(fectus)] civitatium [Pirustarum]m*, meaning the Siculotae, Cerauni and Scirtones, must remain problematical in his oppinion.

Wilkes suggests that Pirustae occupied once a large area including that of Pljevlja. It was the tribe mentioned by Livy as a segment of the Dassareti who were, along with the Taulantii and Daorsi guaranteed *immunitas* (tax exemption) in the settlement of 167 BC. The trouble among Roman allies in Illyricum in 54 BC. was settled by Caesar (BG V, 1,5) and Pirustae were defeated straightaway Octavianus in 33 BC. (Appian, III, 16). Wilkes concludes that Pirustae were a large people inhabiting a great mountanious region inckluding northern Montenegro and eastern Bosnia and because of that the Romans found impracticable to organized a *civitas* of Pirustae, and therefore they do not appear in Pliny's list of the Narona conventus. There is no need, in his opinion, to suggest that Pirustae as a whole have ever changed their territory between 167 BC. and 9, but there seems little doubt that a substantial proportion of the Dalmatian who were transported in the mining district in Alburnus Maior in Dacia in the early second century AD were from Pirustae.

Judging by the names on later Latin inscriptions in a settlement near Komini, the Celtic component of the population was also significant. Wilkes thinks that it confirms the information about the Pirustae as a Pannonian tribe.[29] They could have been the neighbors of the Celtic Scordisci in Pannonia. Ptolemy, writing in the late second century lists in his *Geography* the tribes, strongholds and cities in the provinces, along the Sava and the Danube and those far away from them.

There is no doubt that the hypothesis about three *civitates* instead of that of the Pirustae, or their part, and about the Siculotae in the Pljevlja area is attractive. However, it is difficult to accept it because the territory inhabited by the Scirtones, Cerauni and Siculotae at the time when the ancient authors recorded them, cannot be identified with any certainty. In other words, the ancient authors say nothing that could refer to a tribe in the Lim or the Ćehotina valley and their tributaries. Of the known tribes, the Pirustae who inhabited the south of the province of Dalmatia are the nearest to the Lim and Ćehotina valley. It is possible that they migrated from their territory to the Lim valley. Judging by the name repertory, the Delmatae could be also associated with the *municipium* near Komini. It remains to be seen whether the archaeological remains and nomenclature preserved traces of the pre-Roman population in the Pljevlja area.

---

[27] Alföldy, Bevölkerung 58.
[28] Wilkes, Dalmatia, 173 f.
[29] Strabo, VII 5,5 includes them among Pannonian tribes.

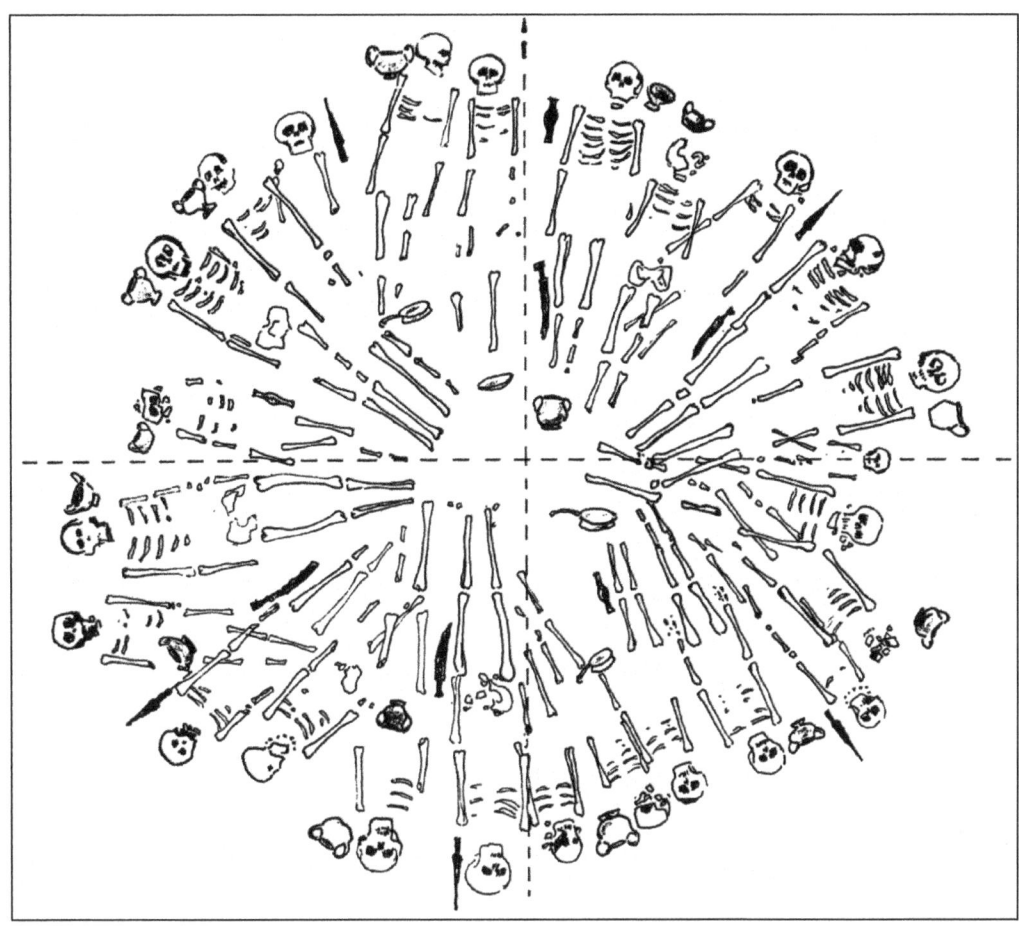

Fig. 3: Tumulus at Krajčinoviči near Priboj

b) ARCHAEOLOGICAL ARGUMENTS

Investigation of pre-Roman localities in the Ćehotina valley and the Lim basin

The crucial problem in archaeological investigations in the Lim basin and Western Serbia represents the broken continuity of cultures, and the lack of it from the 6th or 5th century BC. to proto-history and the arrival of the Romans. There is a hiatus in the archaeological material from the end of the 6th century until the last two centuries BC. as is proved by the until now undertaken archaeological investigations in the central Balkan area, including the Lim valley. Discovered graves in Western Serbia belong to the early Iron Age as the last stage before the Roman arrival. This phenomenon is present in many of investigated localities.[30]

It must be addmited that only a few pre-historical sites have been investigated around Pljevlja and Prijepolje. For the time being, there are no reliable pre-historical finds from Pljevlja that could be dated to the period between the 6th century BC. and the arrival of the Romans. Four tumuli of Illyrian warriors were discovered in Gotovuša near Pljevlja, dated to the 6th and the beginning of the 5th century;[31] the investigated Iron Age tumulus at the Savin Lakat site on Jabuka between Pljevlja and Prijepolje belongs to the same period and speaks of the same problem.[32] Settlements Komini near Pljevlja and Kolovrat near Prijepolje are much younger and according to the archaeological excavations so far, did not come into being before the first century BC. What happened there in the meantime cannot be determined on the basis of the material brought to light by excavations at these sites. Systematic excavations have been modest in scope and conducted mostly in urban necropolises. It can be assumed that some ethnical groups disappeared from the Lim basin during conflicts between tribes referred to by the ancient authors or that there were major ethnic migrations caused by war, disease and hunger. It is hard to believe that the Lim basin remained waste and uninhabited during several centuries.

Another phaenomenon in this region, in the upper Lim valley, represents the tumulus in Krajčinovići, some 15 km south-west of Priboj and 35 km on the north of Pljevlja. The tumulus was on the Illyrian territory, but the La Tène grave goods from the locality seems to indicate

---

[30] M. Zotović, Arheološki i etnički problemi bronzanog i gvozdenog doba zapadne Srbije, Beograd, 1985, 11 and 128. His researches concern the large area from the river Drina on the west to the mountain Jelica, Dragačevo and Golija mountain on the east, Vlašić mountain and rivers Iader and Kolubara on the north; on the south he researches the region of Priboj, Prijepolje, Nova Varoš, Sjenica and Novi Pazar.

[31] Zotović, 126.

[32] M. Lazić, Humka iz Bronzanog doba na lokalitetu Savin lakat kod Prijepolja, Arhaika 1, 2007, 109-127.

Fig. 4: Tumulus at Otilovići near Pljevlja

Fig. 5: Grave in the city cemeteries at Komini

Fig. 6: Urn from the Roman cemeteries at Komini

that the Celtic ethnic component in the Lim basin from around the second century BC. should not be discounted. Finds in the tumulus are of Celtic origin or were made under the Celtic technical influence as shown by the pottery, jewellery and weapons found in it. Burials in tumuli are not characteristic of the Celts in the Balkans and this fact alone makes it difficult to relate the Krajčinovići finds with the Scordisci who lived in Pannonia in the historical period. Nonetheless, the material, analogous with some finds outside the Illyrian territory, such as, for instance, a tumulus in Oltenia attributed to Celts, and the manner of burial in a stratum at Gomolava in Srem permit this hypothesis.[33] Close parallels with bracelets with snake heads are found in the material from the Danube basin, the Židovar fortress dated to La Tène II and a Celtic fortification near Rospi Ćuprija in Belgrade. They are also found in the La Tène I archaeological material in Gallia. For the time being, any discussion about whether and how the Scordisci, if they were in question, extended to the Central Balkans cannot go beyond hypotheses.

The fate of the Illyrians and other Central Balkan peoples in that part of the Central Balkans from the 5th century BC. until the Romans remains a mystery.

Archaeological material from tombs in Roman necropolises I and II in Komini and the pre-Roman population

Fig. 7: Grave in the city cemeteries at Komini

Recent excavations of two cemeteries from the Roman period in Komini do not resolve either the issue about the continuity between the pre-Roman population and the Roman city. The archaeological as well as the onomastic material from the Roman settlements refers primarily to the population of the Roman town. It does not go beyond the first century BC, that is after the Roman arrival in this part of the Balkans. Nonetheless, this material, important for the study of the population during the Romans can, to a certain degree, help in the study of earlier periods because it contains elements of non-Roman cultures even if there were other factors which affected the population in the Roman time, including transfers from areas sometimes rather remote.

Two necropolises found in Komini are partly contiguous and it can be assumed that the later one (Necropolis II) followed up on the earlier necropolis (Necropolis I). Burials in the Necropolis I were performed throughout the first century and later on its western edge. The finds belong to the time from the end of the first century BC. to the first decades of the fourth century. Burials were performed without a particular order that could be identifiable today and without inscribed tombstones. Necropolis II is in a number of ways different from Necropolis I. Firstly, it is younger; secondly, the graves and tombs follow a certain order and thirdly, it is much richer in grave objects than Necropolis I. It is made of several fenced family cemeteries. The excavations of 1965-67 brought to light eight such fenced areas, each with a different type of tombs. The graves and tombs were on the terraces cut into the slopes of Beli Breg hill in the south-north direction. Two terraces with a passage which the tombs faced were also discovered. Subsequent investigations resulted in more material and a number of graves and tombs.

Note should be made of the observations of A. Cermanović-Kuzmanović about the pre-Roman element in the material from the Komini necropolises found in particular during the investigation of Necropolis I. They are summed up in a short article.[34] She attributes a group of graves marked as graves type I in Necropolis I to the native population. Of 41 urns with the ashes of the deceased, only 6 were done on the wheel; the others were shaped by hand and their shapes bring to mind those belonging to the Halstadt period. She sees the similarity with the pre-historical manner of burial in yet another thing: the urns were surrounded by stone wreaths or stone slabs. A. Cermanović-Kuzmanović relates the rectangular stone urns to the local tradition, close to the familiar form of Iapodes' urns.

A. Cermanović-Kuzmanović finds the parallel burials of burnt remains in the urn covered by a slab as of the middle of the first millennium over a wide area in the Illyrian territory, with the Iapodes who buried the dead in urns covered by a stone wreath and later on by a stone slab, the Drina valley where there are tumuli with urns fenced by stones and covered with a plate, Southern Serbia and Northern Kosovo (Gornja Stražara, Brnjica, Karagač). A knife stuck next to the urn is a characteristic feature of burials in Necropolis I in Komini. She notes that the same custom is found in the graves of burnt remains of the dead in Donja Dolina in Bosnia.

Some types of crude pottery in the material from both necropolises are common to peoples in a wide area inhabited by Illyrian tribes. Such urns are found in Iapodes and Delmatae necropolises from the Halstadt B period (Kompolje) and later in many places (Donja Drina, Bihać, Jezerine, around the source of the Cetina). The nearest parallel for a large group comprising pottery vessels, shallow or deep conical bowls, is found in the pottery discovered in Iapodes' necropolises. Finely structured chalices with two handles are modelled, in

---

[33] M. Zotović, 130 f.

[34] A. Cermanović-Kuztmanović, *Vorrömische Elemente in der Kultur des Municipium S... im Dorfe Komini*, Živa antika 30, iz 1980, 227-232.

Figs. 8-10: Urnes from the Roman cemeteries at Komini

terms of shape and decoration, after La Tène pottery. A. Cermanović-Kuzmanović draws the attention to the parallels in the Celtic pottery and the finds in Donja Dolina dating to 250-125 BC. Some examples of pinted pottery found in the younger necropolis at Komini is also of La Tène origin. In Pannonia, it is associated mostly with La Tène tradition and was made in the second century. In Dalmatia, and in Komini, it appeared later and should be dated to the 3rd century. Cermanović-Kuzmanović dated the painted pottery in Komini to the third century because it was found alongside a glass bowl, originally from Cologne (p. 230).

In the opinion of Cermanović-Kuzmanović the Iapodes element in the jewellery is less visible. The fibulae types were predominantly imported from the Alpine area (*aucissa fibulae*). The Iapodes influence is noted in pins and fibulae decorated with the golden thread. This type of fibulae is found in the territory inhabited by the Japodes during Phase III at the Jezerine site dated to 360-250 BC. A. Cermanović-Kuzmanović points out at the Iapodes parallels and La Tène elements in the material from the Pljevlja necropolises and holds that they may not be ignored when interpreting the material from the graves in Komini. However, the mode of burial and the grave material can show the relationship of the population of the Pljevlja *municipium* with a wide area including the Delmatae and the Iapodes, but not with a specific people. The onomastic material, predominantly Illyrian, indicates the same thing.

The analysis in A. Cermanović-Kuzmanović's article refers to the time when the Cemetery I in Komini begins, that means prior to the first century BC. Nonetheless, it contains conclusions suggesting further investigation. The excavations covered large areas and resulted in a huge amount of archaeological material. Among it, none can be dated to the time prior to the 1st century BC. In the Roman town one can talk about two or more ethnic components, but the ethnic origin of the pre-Roman population in a wide area around Pljevlja and Prijepolje is still ignored. The Illyrian material predominates in the graves and there is no doubt that a large portion of the population in the Roman period was of Illyrian origin. An important aspect of the archaeological investigations of A. Cermanović-Kuzmanović is that she demonstrated the Celtic component in the settlement's material culture. Only further excavations in the area could show whether these are individual finds or the true Celtic element in the Ćehotina valley culture. Some names on Roman tombstones indicate the Celtic component among the population in the settlements near Komini and Kolovrat. The onomastic analysis allows moving a step further in the investigation of the origins of the population of the Roman town near Komini.

*

Literary and archaeological evidence indicate the following conclusion: literary sources offer no information permitting to relate a tribe reliably to the area of the Lim valley and the Upper Drina. It is impossible to determine the tribal origin of the archaeological material. It is indubitably the Illyrian territory and the Illyrians were the principal population in the Lim and Drina basins. It is possible that the Pirustae extended as far, but they must have been branches of the tribe at the time of the Pirustae expansion before Gentius's Illyrian troops were defeated in 168 BC. Strabo's claim that they were a Pannonian tribe would permit to look for them even north of the Albanian mountains. Information provided by various authors probably does not relate to the same period. One cannot truly expect them to live simultaneously in the south, next to the Dassareti and extend as far as the Pannonian tribes, including those which had moved there from Gallia. They possibly disappeared from northern Montenegro even before the defeat of the Dalmatian-Pannonian revolt and left no trace behind them. For the time being, the theory about the Pirustae in the Lim basin and the Ćehotina valley during the Romans does not go beyond modern scientific combinations.

The archaeological research has brought to light a phenomenon: the excavations in Western Serbia and around Prijepolje did not produce a stratum or material which could be dated to the time between the end of 6th century BC. and the Roman arrival. The theory about the 6th – 2nd centuries' hiatus is based on tumuli investigated in the broad Central Balkan area. The number of recorded tumuli around Pljevlja and Prijepolje is undoubtedly large,[35] but few of them have been investigated and it can be expected that future excavations with tell us with more certainty whether there was a break between the Late Iron Age and the Later Halstadt period. Investigations in a wide area around Krajčinovići near Priboj seem to indicate another possible conclusion: a people of Celtic origin who pushed out the Illyrians could have inhabited the area in Halstadt. If that was the case, being immigrants, they could not have been many and must have represented a thin stratum. It is possible that this fertile valley was repopulated only by the Romans when they brought colonists from elsewhere, or possibly soldiers of auxiliary detachments after finishing their service. Evans assumed that the Halstadt stratum exists on the hill of Sveti Ilija (Ilijino brdo) where native Illyrian names appear on the inscriptions.[36]

c) ONOMASTIC ARGUMENTS: NATIVE NAMES ON ROMAN INSCRIPTIONS IN KOMINI AND KOLOVRAT SETTLEMENTS

The native, non-Roman population in Roman settlements in Komini and Kolovrat left a clear mark on the nomenclature in the Roman inscriptions. The onomastic analysis allows moving a step further in the investigation of the origins of the population of both, the Roman town in Komini near Pljevlja and the settlement in Kolovrat.

The investigations is based on native names from Municipium S. and its surroundings, from Kolovrat and Ivangrad. The following names are preserved:

Native names in Municipium S( )
Aplis (T.Aur.)
Apla
Aplis Aurel. Arguranus
Argenianus (Aur.Maximus)
Arguriana (Aur. Titulla)
Baezo
Bessus
Brizidia (Statius Victor)
Cambria (Aur. Titulla)
[---]Cambrianus
Cato Statariae Tur.
Durus
Fusca Anae
Iaro Arvi
Lavius
Maxillo (?)
Nantius Sexti
Panto (Aurelia) (2)
Panto
Pinsus
Plares (Aur.)
Plarens (Aurelius)
Pletor
Scaevianus
Tata
Terens (together with Vendo)
Titus

---
[35] M. Lazić, Topografija i tipologija praistorijskih tumula u Srbiji i Crnoj Gori, Beograd 1988. Usefull informations about the tumuli and other monuments in the Pljevlje and Prijepolje area could be found in the small book written by the amateur Joko V. Knežević, Iz daleke prošlosti Pljevaljskog kraja, Pljevlje 1979.

[36] Evans, Antiquarian Researches, 31 ff.

Titus Apri
Turo Pinsi (Aur.)
Turus (T.Aur.)
Vendo (Aur.) (2)
Vendo
Verzo, Verzalio

Ilijino brdo:
Bessus (Ae.)
Germanus
Testo (Aurelia)
Tito (Aur.)
Tritano (Aur.)
Vendo (Aur.)

Native names in the Roman settlement at Kolovrat
Ana Severina: Užički zbornik 18, 1989. 4
Titus Anae Codalianus: Spomenik 98, 1941-1948, no. 333
Aplis Pantoni: Godišnjak CBI 12. 1975, 98, no. 3
Bazo: Užićki zbornik 18, 1989, 3
Bessio (Statius): Užički zbornik 18, 1989, 4
Cato: Godišnjak CBI 12, 1975, no. 3
Clemio: Godišnjak CBI 12, 1975, no. 3
Delmana: Arch. Jug. 19,1978, 46-47
Dusona: Godišnjak CBI 12, 1975, no. 3
Lavo (Statia): Godišnjak CBI 12, 1975, 100, no. 8
Lavius (Aur.): Godišnjak CBI 12, 1975, 99, no. 5 and Arch. Jug. 19, 47
Madita (Aur.): Godišnjak CBI 12, 1975, 99, no. 5
Musta: Godišnjak CBI 12, 1975, 98, no. 6
Narensis: Godišnjak CBI 12, 1975, 100, no. 7
Panto; Godišnjak CBI 12, 1975, 98, no. 3
Plares: Arch. Jug. 19, 1978, 46-47
Scenuta: Arch. Jug. 19, 1978, 46-47
Surilla: Godišnjak CBI 12, 1975, 98, no. 6
Suricinus: Godišnjak CBI 12, 18975, 99, no. 5
Tito (Ael.): Starinar 32, 1981, 77, no. 5
Trito: Godišnjak CBI 12, 1975, 98, no. 4
Venuco (Aur.): Godišnjak CBI 12, 1975, 99, no. 5
Vurus: Spomenik 71, 1931, 162, no. 335

The region between Prijepolje on the east and Nova Varoš and Ivangrad on the southwest

Lim valley

Rosulje near Prijepolje: *Belzeius*
Sergejevski, Spomenik SKA 77, 1934, 17, no. 21 (A. et J. Šašel, ILJug. 1731).
Alföldy connects *Belzeius* and the Celtic *Belsus*; Meyer considers the name as Illyric, Rendić, Arh. Jug. 2, 1965, 45 suggests the ethnical meaning.

Toci near Priboj: *Madussa*
Vulić, Spomenik 31, 1931, no. 316 with photo. (A. et J. Šašel, ILJug. 1736). See no. ?.
Alföldy considers the name *Madussa* as *Madu* the Drina river valley, Celtic. See Holder, Altcelt. Sprachsch. II 370 for *Madu*; contrary Katičić, Zur Frage der keltischen und pannonischen Namengebiete im römsichen Dalmatien, Godišnjak CBI 1, 1965, 53-76, thinks that the name shows the typical Illyrian construction.

Seljani: Lavius
Patsch, GZM 6, 1896, 487, no. 49, with drawing fig. 34 and idem, WMBH 4, 1896, 291, no. 49 with drawing of the first three lines (CIL III 13848); Vulić, Spomenik 71, 1931, no. 337 and Spomenik 98, 1941-1948, no. 36 with drawing by Sergejevski (A. et J. Šašel, ILJug. 1962).

Čadinje: Pladomenus, Carvanio, Panto
M. Hoernes, AEM 4, 1880, 197, no. 3b, using imprint by Austrian vice-consul in Pljevlja Müller and completed by A.v. Domaszewski; Evans, Archaeologia 49, 1885, 44 with drawing fig. 21; CIL III 8308. See no. 1b.

Džurovo on the left bank of the river Lim: **Lavianus**
A. Deroko and I. Zdravković, Starinar 1, 1950, 183-184 (A. et J. Šašel, ILJug. 75A).

Derikonjići: Turo
Vulić, Spomenik 71, 1931, no. 331 with photo (A. et J. Šašel, ILJug. 1696).
The name *Turus/Turo* is common in the middle Dalmatian region, Katićić, MDN 282.

The region of Ivangrad

The village **Lužac: Terentoni**
Vulić, Spomenik 71, 1931, no. 12 (A. et J. Šašel ILJug. 1816).

Budimlje: Verzalio
CIL III 13832; Vulić, Spomenik 71, 1931, no. 11 with photo (A. et J. Šašel, ILJug. 1814).

The names allow to discuss the following questions:

– Illyrians and the Delmatae tribe: names and their connection with the pre-Roman substratum in the Ćehotina- and Lim valley – the problem which is not solved neither by the analysis of the literary evidence or by the archaeological researches; People in the Ćehotina valley and the Delmatae: possibility of linking the names in Municipium S. with the determined people or tribes, as were the Delmatae;

– Non-Illyrian native names: Celts and Thracians;

– Similarity and differences: native names in the inscriptions from Komini and in Kolovrat and the population in these two settlements.

When solving the question of the origin of those bearing native names in the Roman settlement near Pljevlja one should make a distinction among, first, the Illyrian names appearing in a wider area, then those in the Lim basin and its vicinity and, finally, those appearing only in Pljevlja or only in Prijepolje.

Illyrians in the central Balkan region; natives in the inscriptions in Municipium and the Delmatae

There is no doubt that the Roman town grew in an area considered Illyrian and that a large part of the population, judging by their names, was of Illyrian origin. Most non-

Roman names in the inscriptions from Pljevlja and its whereabouts are Illyrian,[37] as it is considered, typical of middle Dalmatian region.[38] The names of this group are found on Roman inscriptions in a large area stretching out from Dalmatia and the central part of the Adriatic coast to the Central Balkans and the Morava basin.

The onomastic similarities between Delmatae and the region of Pljevlje and Prijepolje could mean that some names were common to a large area inhabited by the Illyrians. That they existed is indicated by the appearance of *Bato* as a name among Breuci in Srem and among Delmatae during the Dalmatian-Pannonian revolt. It should mean that there was an Illyrian substratum in the west Balkans which survived until the historical time.

The nomenclature in Roman inscriptions in Pljevlja and Prijepolje eloquently speaks about the ties with the Delmatae. The comparison can be made with inscriptions in the coastal area of the province of Dalmatia, mostly in Rider and Vrlike. Those names could have existed in the area between the Adriatic coast and the Lim basin, but the absence of inscriptions in the rest of the area precludes any other comparison. One should bear in mind that there are no major concentrations of the epigraphic material in the inland part of the Balkan Peninsula, between the Adriatic coast and Lim valley.

It is not truly possible to compare and seek parallels either in other parts of the Illyrian world on the east of the region. A larger concentration of monuments with Illyrian and other local names exists only in Dardania, in Kosovo, in the Central Illyrian area and in the area of Užice and Požega in west Serbia. Names from the Roman inscriptions from Kosovo area have no parallels in the names in the inscriptions from the Roman settlements near Pljevlja. Kosovo inscriptions confirm local names, which do not exist on monuments in the Lim basin. Rare onomastic similarities with the region of Pljevlja lead to the area around Požega and Užice, i.e. the territory of the municipium Malvesatium. *Catula* is a name which, together with *Cato-onis* and *Catta* appears in a large area: in Iader, Pljevlja, Bajina Bašta and Karan.[39]

Few names in the inscriptions from Municipium can be associated with the South Illyrian group. Only *Plares* could fall into this last group of names.

There is no doubt that a large number of names on Pljevlja and Prijepolje inscriptions have numerous parallels in the Delmatae territory. The names common to the Delmatae area and the Central Balkan area around Pljevlja and Prijepolje could be the remains of the same substratum, but onomastic similarities in areas hundreds of kilometres apart could also be explained as a result of ethnic movements during pre-Roman centuries or resettlemens from coastal areas inland under the Romans. G. Alföldy significantly contributed to the study. His considerations about the origin of the population should also include the names from a broad Central Balkan area. In his article *Die Namengebung der Urbevölkerung in der römischen Provinz Dalmatia, Beträge zur Namenforschung* 15, 1964. Alföldy then proceeds to single out from this territorially very large group those names which would be typical of certain tribes: the Japodes, Liburni and Delmatae. He associated some names with the Ardiei, Pirustae and some smaller tribes which could be included among the southern Illyrian tribes. The most numerous are the names confirmed in many inscriptions in the territory inhabited by the Delmatae. Alföldy includes there names such as *Carvanius, Germanus, Panto, Pinsus, Stataria, Testo, Titto, Tritano, Turo, Vendo, Verzaius*. He holds that some of the names on the monuments from the area of Pljevlja are typical of the area inhabited by Delmatae: *Carvanius* is an Illyrian name, originally, in Alföldy's view, a gentile name known in the form of *Carvius* in Rider and as *Carvus; Turus* is confirmed also in Rider and Siculi; *Pladomenus*, confirmed on several inscriptions in Rider and other central Dalmatian localities, e.g. Novi Pazar.[40] *Lavius* and similar names would fall into the same group in view of the number of confirmed examples in Rider. *Statius* and *Staticus* are shared by both areas; *Aplis Staticus* and *Turus Staticus Tritti* in Rider, *Celso Statica Bubanti[--], Staticu[us* or *– a] P[l]atoris* f., GZM 6, 1951, pp. 59-60 and in Trogir area, VHAD 55, 1953, 254 and *Statius, Staticus, Stataria* in Komini near Pljevlja, *Sex. Statius Restitutus*, husband *Aurelia Testo*, CIL III 8326, *Statius Victor Brizidia*, CIL III 8302, *Statius Bessio* in Prijepolje, Užički zbornik 18, 1989, 4, *Statia Am?[,]ena*, Zbornik Filozofskog fakulteta Beograd, XI-1, 1970, n. 2. It could also be an indication in the identification of the origin of peoples in the Pljevlja area.

The match between the Delmatae and the people in Lim basin group is reflected also in the nomeclature formulae. The peoples in these two non-contiguous areas share not only the individual names, such as *Apla, Cato* etc., but also the onomastic formula. One of the telling examples is *Cato Statariae Turi* on a Komini inscription and *Turo Statariae Turo f.* in Sikuli on the Delmatae territory, Bul.dalm. 34, 1911, p. 50 (ILJug. 193). The onomastic practice is a factor of sociological rather than linguistic nature. Rendić-Miočević includes some names in Pljevlja inscriptions in the group of simple names (e.g. Aurelia Vendo) or those with a two-member formula which could also be a reflection of the social structure when an individual is associated either with a narrow group (*gens*) or an extended community (tribe).[41] It is unlikely that the name or the onomastic formula alone would be taken over without corresponding social forms. In a stratum so Romanised that it took over the Latin alphabet, the Roman onomastic formula was accepted and in it the gentile name was the most important. It is, however, chosen, as a rule, after an emperor (*Aelius, Aurelius*) whereas for the locals, the old name took the place of the *cognomen*. The new name on the inscriptions was

---

[37] A, Mayer, Die Sprache der alten Illyrier, Wien, 1957, passim.
[38] R. Katičić, Das mitteldalmatische Namengebiet, Živa Antika 12, 1963 (= MDN), 255-292.
[39] Katičić, MDN 266.

[40] See R. Katičić, MDN 173.
[41] D. Rendić-Miočević, Ilirska onomastika na latinskim natpisima Dalmacije, 1948.

Table I

Name	Pljevlje	Prijepolje	Lim valley	MDN*	Rider
Ana	+	+		?	
Aplis, Apla	+	+		+	+
Apris?	+				
Argenianus	+				
Baizo, Baezo	+	+			
Belzeius			+		
Bessus	+				
Brizidia	+				
Cambria, Cambrianus	+				
Carvanio		+			
Cato	+	+		+	
Clemio, Celemio	+	+			
Dardana		+			
Delmana		+			
Dusona		+			
Durus		+			
Germanus	+				
Iarito	+			+	
Lavo, Lavius		+	+		
Lautus		+			
Madita		+			
Maxillo	+				
Musta		+			
Nantius	+				+
Narensis		+			
Panto	+	+		+	+
Pladomenus		+	+		+
Plares	+	+	+		
Pletor	+				
Pinsus	+				+
Scaevianus	+				
Scenuta		+			
Stataria	+				
Tata	+				
Teres	+				
Testo	+				
Titto, Tito	+	+			
Tritano	+				+
Turus, Turo	+		+		
Vendo	+	+			+
Venuco		+			
Verzo, Verzaius	+	+	+		+
Vurus	+				

* Middle Dalmatian Names.

brought into harmony with the Roman onomastic formula. The Illyrian form of a one name or the onomastic formula of the name with patronymic, such as *Iarito Arvi*, was rarely kept. The name *Aplis Aureli Argirinus*, with the imperial gentile name as patronymic shows a significant deviation from the usual formula among Romanised Illyrians. He was probably individually tied to his old *gens* as shown by the two Illyrian names: *Aplis* and *Argurinus*. The third, the imperial gentile name, took the place of the patronymic as a sign of integration into the Roman community.

Alföldy excludes the possibility that it was one people which inhabited the territory from the Adriatic coast to the Tara and Lim rivers at the same time. The similarity with the Delmatae nomenclature even in the formal sense (two-member onomastic formula) leads Alföldy also to conclude that the people in the Pljevlja-Prijepolje area moved from the Delmatae area. In his opinion the similarity could be explained by the transfers of tribes under the Romans rather than by the ethnic movements in pre-historical times. He suggests that the Siculi who inhabited the region between Salona and Tragurion have been moved by the Romans in order to secure the land for the veterans to the region of Pljevlje and Prijepolje. They have to replace in the northern Montenegro the Pirustae who were weakened in the wars with the Romans during the Delmatian uprising. His crucial argument is the name *Municipium S[icu[lo(tarum)*, as he reconstructed the damaged text in the inscription no. **1b**.[42]

Names parallel to those in Pljevlja and Prijepolje can be found primarily in Rider, Vrlike and other settlements of the middle Dalmatian onomastic area along the coast, as shown by the table. A large number of inscriptions have survived there. Onomastic similarities between the Roman settlementsin Pljevlja and Prijepolje and those of the Delmatae are beyond doubt, but some of those names are also found on inscriptions in a large part of the Central Balkans. Of the names confirmed in Pljevlja and Prijepolje: *Apla, Aplo* and the like, *Lavius, Panto*, and *Vendo* have been confirmed by a large number of examples in Rider; *Pinsus* in Rider and Vrlike; *Cato* and *Cattus* appear in Pljevlja but also and Bajina Bašta in Drina valley on the north-east, and in Iader, *Iaritus* in Pljevlja and Bihać, *Pladomenus* in a large area from Rider to Novi Pazar, *Vendo* in Rider, Bihać in the west Bosnia and Pljevlja; *Tritanus* in Promona, Pljevlja and Rider. *Tatta* is another name confirmed in a large area of the Central Balkans: in addition to Pljevlja it has been confirmed in Karan, *Tattaia* in Požega in West Serbia.[43]

Celts

The big majority of the names in Lim and Ćehotina valley is Illyrian. However some names this region could be Celtic rather than Illyrian.[44] The appearance of Celtic names on monuments in the Komini settlement is undoubtedly also important. They could be associated with the pre-Roman substratum. G. Alföldy believes that they could have been the Scordisci.[45] He deserves tribute for singling out Celtic names in that group. He includes among the Celtic names in Pljevlja and Prijepolje the following: *Arvus, Belzeius, Cambrius, Iaritus, Lautus* and *Madussa*. In his view they could be associated with the Scordisci who arrived in the Balkan Peninsula in the fourth century BC., or with Iapodes who are an Illyrian-Celtic people or an Illyrian people influenced by the Celts. In another article published the same year, *Des territoire occupies par les Scordisques*,[46] he relates the Celtic names on inscriptions in the area stretching from the Drina to the Morava rivers: *Aioia, Baeta, Bidua, Calvus, Catta, Dussona, Enena, Laca, Madusa, Matisa, Nindia, Sarnus, Totia* and in north-western Moesia: *Aia, Bella* and *Opusia*, to the Scordisci, a Celtic tribe which extended over a wide area from the lower Sava to the Iron Gates under the name of Small and Big Scordisci. Alföldy believes that during the Roman time administrative entity called *civitas Scordiscorum* existed in South-eastern Srem, the Celegeri and Tricornienses in Moesia and the Dindarae in Dalmatia were parts of the same tribe. Analogies in Gallia and other Celtic lands should confirm Celtic origin of the quoted names. During their foray into the Balkans at the time of the big migration in the fourth century BC, the Celts could have followed the Sava and Drina valleys to reach the central part of the Balkan Peninsula. The names in the lower Sava area and along the Danube between the mouths of the Sava and the Morava could be attributed to the Scordisci, a Celtic tribe. The tribe was highly mobile and in its forays to the south they reached Macedonia and even Greece. They could have extended as far as the central Balkan area around Pljevlja. The presence of Celtic names in Drina and Lim valley could be explained by speculating about a secondary Celtic migration from the Sava Basin or about a Celtic tribe which separated from the main wave when they moved to the Balkan Peninsula in the late fourth century BC and ended up in the south, far from the Sava. One should not forget the Iapudes either: they are an Illyrian-Celtic people or an Illyrian people which suffered Celtic influence.

The archaeological finds from the tumulus on this place encourage further investigations in the same direction, especially as Celtic parallels might be found for some material in Necropolis I in Komini. La Tène material prevails, also in a tumulus Krajčinovići near Priboj.[47]

Among Celtic names in Municipium G. Alföldy, includes *Belzeius*, associating it with *Belsus, Belsa* (Holder I 396 and III 844), *Madussa* and *Lautus* in the same area and *Cambrius, Iaritus* and *Argurianus* in the inscriptions from

---

[42] Alföldy, Bevölkerung, 57 ff.
[43] Cf. Alföldy, BNF p. 96.
[44] G. Alföldy, Die Namengebung der Urbevölkerung in Delmatien, Beitrage zur Namenforschung 15, 1964, 99.
[45] G. Alföldy, Les territoires occuppés par les Scordisques, Acta ant. hung. 12, 107-127. Cf. and Bevölkerung, 56. On Scordisci see F. Papazoglu, The Central Balkan Tribes in pre-Roman times, Triballi, Autariatae, Dardanians, Scordisci and Moesians, Amsterdam, 1978, 271-392.
[46] Acta. Ant. Hung. XII, 1964, 124.
[47] M. Zotović, Arheološki i etnički problemi bronzanog i gvozdenog doba zapadne Srbijre, 1985, 100 ff.

the city Necropolis II.[48] The name *Verzalio*, confirmed also at the urban Necropolis I in Komini warrants attention. *Dassius Verzo* on a wax tablet from Alburnus Maior in Dacia was a Pirusta ex Cavieretio (IDR I 36). G. Alföldy thinks it is a Delmatae name and Katičić, SIN 284 holds that it is a south Illyrian name. This could be a spoor leading to Pirustae in the southern Illyrian area, who could have extended to the Lim basin before the Romans. This name does not suffice to affirm that they remained in the environs of the Roman city in the second and third century, but does not rule out this hypothesis. *Plarens* and *Terens*, found also in Pljevlja, appear also on Dacian wax tablets, but as the tribe they belonged to is ignored, they cannot be used to confirm a hypothesis of this kind.

Thracians

Thracian element is not possibly to distinguish clearly in the Roman settlements in this region. There are also some Thracian names in the both settlements, Komini near Pljevlja and Kolovrat near Prijepolje, but they are few. *Bessus* and *Teres*, or *Plares* in Pljevlja and *Bessio* in Prijepolje might be of Thracian origin. They could have represent immigrants from Thracian lands rather then the vestige of a situation long time past and the Thracian ethnic stratum in this part of the Balkan Peninsula. Katičić, MDN, 264, believes that *Bessus* belongs to native names in Central Balkan area. He includes also the name *Teres*, derived from *Terent-*, among Illyrian names and thinks it should be different from a similar Thracian name *Teres*.[49] Thracian names *Besus* in Plevlja and *Bessio* in Prijepolje could also be ethnic names. The *Bessi* are a Thracian tribe but they are also mentioned as one of the tribes which fought against Octavianus in Illyricum in 35-33 BC. It is interesting to note that *Bessus-a* appears only in Dalmatia, Gallia Narbonensis, Noricum, Upper Moesia; *Besius* has been confirmed in *Gallia Lugdunensis*, but the name is missing in Thrace and Dacia.

Thracian substratum in the Central Balkans has not been confirmed archaeologically.[50] Since the inscriptions are from the Roman period, the hypothesis that they belonged to immigrants is quite possible and plausible.

Similarities and differences

The research conducted so far considered the names from these two settlements together with those from Prijepolje as one group. The names from the Pljevlja and Prijepolje areas with the largest concentration of native names in the inland part of the province of Dalmatia Alföldy singled out, as a separate group.[51] He believes that the names from the two Roman settlements in Komini near Pljevlja and in Kolovrat near Prijepolje were part of an onomastic whole. Nomenclature reflects also the ethnic situation. It would be logical to conclude that the area was inhabited by one and the same people. This is justifiable because a large number of names appear in both settlements some 30 km apart from each other. Most of them are considered middle Illyrian, appearing on Delmatae and Liburni inscriptions and those in the Lim basin. On the other hand, one should not disregard the fact that some non-Roman names are not shared by both settlements and that they are confirmed only in Pljevlja or only in Prijepolje. There are names which appear only in the inscription from Pljevlja as *Argenianus, Belzeius, Bessus, Brizidia, Cambria-Cambrius, Durus, Germanus, Iarito, Maxillo, Pinsus, Teres, Testo, Turus*. Some of them are defined as Celtic (*Belzeius, Camria, Maxillo*), others as Thracian (Bessus, Teres?). Only in the Roman settlement near Prijepolje appear *Carvanius* or *Carvanio* (Ćadinje), *Dardana, Delmana, Dusona, Madita, Narensis, Scaevianus, Scenuta, Vurus*. Ethnic name *Dardana, Delmana, Narensis* are attested in Kolovrat.

Native names in the inscriptions from Komini and in those from Kolovrat show that these two settlements have much in common. However the names in one or another case lead to the question whether it was there the same people. The table I does not justify the procedure common so far in the study of the population to consider the Roman settlements near Pljevlja and Prijepolje as a single onomastic area and thus the people living there as a single ethnic entity of the same origin; secondly, the names common to both settlements are those of the middle dalmatian, used over a large area from the Adriatic Sea to the Drina and further east, to Novi Pazar and qualified by R. Katičić as the Mitteldalmatische Namengebiet.

*

The onomastic investigations brought to following conclusions:

1. The names in the inscriptions from Pljevlja and Prijepolje are considered as belonging the middle Dalmatian group of names

2. They have close parallels with the names considered Dalmatian.

3. Some names on the Pljevlja inscriptions are Celtic.

4. Thracian names are also found on inscriptions there and in Kolovrat, albeit seldom.

5. Names on Pljevlja and Prijepolje reflect some difference.

An important fact in the consideration of the origin of the population in the Lim basin and the Ćehotina valley is that some of the names on the monuments are not found outside the area and it can be assumed that they belonged to natives before the arrival of the Romans and possible systematic transfers from other places inhabited by the Illyrians. Such conclusion is, for the time being, based

---

[48] BNF 15, p. 97.
[49] Katičić, p. 277.
[50] As has been suggested by K. Patsch, Thrakische Spuren an der Adria, JÖAI 10, 1907, 169-174 (the same in Serbian Tracki tragovi na Adriji, GZM 1907, 463.467). Against this supposition F. Papazoglu, Sur quelques noms "thraces" en Illyrie, Godišnjak XII CBI, knj. 10, 1974, 59-72, basing her consideration on the study of the names in Dardania.
[51] BNF p. 98-102.

only on the analysis of the onomastic material. Archaeological confirmation is missing.

The pre-Roman native stratum in the Pljevlja and Prijepolje area left little trace in the archaeological material. It could be assumed the same substratum stretching over a very large area, traces of which remain in the coastal area and inland. The names in the inscriptions from a larger area, even if few, could be mirroring the situation before the arrival of the Romans better than those in an urban settlement. However, symilarities in the nomeclature between the Delmatae and those who lived in settlements near Komini and Kolovrat could be due to the migration of the part of the population from the Delmatae territory to Lim and Cehotina valley under the Romans. Finally, the names known only in one of the two settlements could suggest that the population, or its part, in these two neighbouring settlements was not the same.

The analysis of the onomastic material seems to indicate that one must count with a strong Illyrian ethnic element in the population of a large area as well as with other ethnic groups, notably the Celts. The Thracian ethnic component should not be excluded either, but the Thracian names, few in number, need not be associated with the stratum of the native population. Therefore, the population must have been mixed.

Finally, in addition to the information obtained through the analysis of other sources, the monuments themselves, ornamentation and portraits of the deceased show that there were at least two different ethnic components in the Roman city, one of which was Roman. Anthropological differences can be observed in portraits represented on steles in the both settlements: they seem to indicate the presence of different peoples or different components of a people, which mixed. The portraits on the monuments in the environs are indicative of the same style, but, one would say, not the same anthropological features. Even if rendered on the basis of identical portrait models, one group represents people with oval, plump faces found on most Roman monuments, and the other shows people with pronounced cheekbones making the face look triangular, with prominent cheekbones and chins. The Phrygian cap on some monuments in Athis can hardly be associated with the onomastic material.

It would seem that the population consisted largely of immigrants. Its characteristic is a rather native component as observed in personal names on tombstones. Illyrian names, in addition to some that may be considered Celtic and occasionally Thracian, survived either as the *cognomen* among those who accepted the Roman *gentilicium* – notably Aurelius – or, more seldom, as the personal name in a one-member formula. Nevertheless one cannot talk about the Illyrians or other ethnic groups which preserved their identity under the Romans, as about separate ethnic groups. Those who were not the citizens of Rome, were organised as *peregrina civitas*. Most of them where Romanised and integrated in the Roman town.

The name could have served as ethnic identification. However, in the Roman city there is no proof that the Illyrians identified themselves as a separate group with their religion, cults and language. No Illyrian deity has been attested in this region until now. It is also rare to find any name without Roman gentile, as testifying to nationality, on the monuments. They could have been peregrines who lived on the city territory, probably organized within the *civitas*. A large number of those bearing Illyrian and other native names, also bear Roman gentile names after the 2nd century emperors. Women with Illyrian names are confirmed on the inscriptions even in such distinguished Roman families as the Paconii.

Figs. 11-12: Portraits on the monuments in the city Cemetery II

Figs. 13-17: Portraits on the monuments in the city Cemetery II

III. ROMAN TOWN IN THE REGION OF PLJEVLJA: MUNICIPIUM S( )

The remains of a large Roman settlement were discovered at present day Pljevlja and its surroundings by travelers in the eighteenth and nineteenth centuries. The emissaries from Ragusa sent to Istanbul in 1702 were the first known travelers to mention Roman antiquities in Pljevlja, the bases of statues, marble columns and inscriptions. Ami Boué, Otto Blau, Arthur Evans and Karl Patsch visited the Turkish city of Pljevlja in the nineteenth and Nikola Vulić in the twentieth century and described and published the inscribed monuments, often immured in the numerous city mosques and the houses of the Turkish begs. Many of the stones from the necropoles, funeral and other monuments, were reused as building material in the later Turkish town of Tashlidja ('stone houses'), present day Pljevlja, founded by the Turkish pasha from Plevna in Bulgaria in 1537, as local tradition says.

The Roman city near Pjevlje occupied the northern edge of the large plain which opens up alongside the Vezičnica stream which cuts though the high mountains of the region and flows into the Ćehotina river. The plain is enclosed by a range of small hills alongside the Vrežišnica stream on the western side. The Mali and Veliki Plijes hills in the middle of the plain were probably inhabited during the Iron Age. No remains from the Roman époque have been discovered on these hills to date. Ilijino brdo, on the southern edge of the plain, with the remains from the Iron Age and the Roman settlement defends the entrance into the valley. The mountains enclosing the Ćehotina and Lim valley give the impression that this region is isolated and cut off from the main communications across the Balkans. In his Antiquarian Research in Illyricum, J.A. Evans describes the position of the Municipium on p. 25: "Beyond Mont Kovač opens the plain of Plevlje the Turkish Tashlidja, containing relicts of Antiquity which mark it as a principal center of Illyrico-Roman civic life. This plain is the only large open space to be found in the mountains for two days' journey on either side and at the same time

Fig. 18: Municipium S( )

Fig. 19: Municipium S( )

Fig. 20: Remains of the Roman city on the bank of the Vezičnica stream

Fig. 21: Remains of the Roman city on the bank of the Vezičnica stream

is the natural crossing point on the highway of communication between the Adriatic coastland and the Moesian and Dardanian staples of which Scupi (Skopia) and Naissus, the modern Niš, may be taken as representatives". The region where the Roman Municipium grew was geographically isolated but connected by a vicinal road to the main communications crossing the Balkans and leading from the Adriatic coast and the Neretva valley to Moesia Superior. Another line of communication along the river Drina leads to Argentares (Srebrnica) in the North and to the Sava valley and further along the river Sava which connected the Balkan provinces to Italy.

The remains of another Roman agglomeration were noted by Evans in the 1880s also on the hill Ilijino Brdo, about 5 km to the southwest of the former on the margins of the plain where a large number of Roman inscriptions have been found. They were reused in the walls and as paving stones in the little church of Sveti Ilija (St. Elias) which gave the name to the hill. Evans observed that the place was initially occupied by the Iron Age people. Since the inscriptions refer to the civic officers, priests, legionaries and citizens, for the most part with Roman names, Evans assumed that Municipium was founded in Hadrian's time here and then enlarged by a fresh settlement of veterans in the age of the Antonines.[52] The Illyrian names, which could be specific to the region, prevailed in the inscriptions.

The Roman town in present day Komini sprang up in the non-urbanized region in the interior of the Roman province of Dalmatia, on the right side of the Vezičnica stream, on the hill slope. The foundations of the city walls and buildings could be recognized in the relief of the fields in the village of Komini. The excavations in the 1970s were carried out for only a short time and were unable to provide enough elements to answer even the elementary question of the size of the civic settlement. Small pieces of the walls and a tower were discovered during the summer excavations in 2009. Judging from the measurement of the space made by geomagnetic investigations the Roman city covered about 40 ha.[53] The best known part of the Roman city are the cemeteries which were excavated by A. Cermanović-Kuzmanović on the western side of the city walls in the 1960s and 70s. She discovered abot than seven hundred graves which will be published by Mira Ružić in volume II of this edition. Two necropoles were in use following one another in a short period of time. The material from the graves; ceramics, brooches, knifes, glass etc. dates from the time between the first and the fourth centuries. We can assume that life in the Roman Municipium lasted during the period framed by the material from the necropoles.

The city territory with small villages and cottages stretches further, to the valley of the river Lim on the West side. Travelers and scientists refer to the isolated monuments on many sites in the immediate surroundings of Pljevlja, such as Koruga, Babiš potok, Podpeć and Radosavce as well as in the entire region between Prijepolje and Pljevlja, in Ljutići and Otilovići not far

---

[52] Evans, Antiquarian Researches, 30f.

[53] As estimated by M. Ružić who conducted the archaeological investigation.

from the Jabuka pass, in Rosulje, in Čadinje and Džurovo, Seljani and Derikonjici, Toci nearby Priboj and other places in the region between Lim and Tara. Some finds suggest the existence of Roman villas or villages in the city surroundings. A big settlement occupied the site of present day Kolovrat on the outskirts of the city of Prijepolje.[54] The municipal status of this agglomeration is not attested in the inscriptions. It could have been one of the sites which was attributed to the Municipium in Komini, whose city territory could have spread out on both sides of the mountain and Jabuka pass, at a distance of 30 km. The discovery of the milestone on the pass Jabuka (no. **41**) proves that the road connecting the two settlements across the mountains was also important in Roman times and probably served as a link to the main road leading to the Adriatic coast.

There are elements in the archaeological material from the cemeteries at Komini indicating the existence of a settlement on the slopes of Bijeli Brijeg in Komini in the first century BC. However the municipium could not be older than the second century AD. There is reason to believe that the majority of the city population came from the coastal region in Dalmatia. What is peculiar in the inscriptions on the funerary monuments is the large number of native names Illyrian in majority, some Celtic and a few Thracian, often bearing the Roman gentile name Aurelius. Romans and those whose names indicate Illyrian origin, lived together.

a) THE NAME OF THE ROMAN MUNICIPIUM IN PRESENT DAY KOMINI

In all modern works concerning the Roman town near Pljevlja it is called Municipium S( ), with different hypothesis as to how to complete its name. The abbreviation S. is recognized as the name of the Municipium in the honorific inscription:

1. Big stone basis of a statue, height 111, width 80, thick 77cm, discovered in the wall of Husein-pasha mosque at Pljevlja. Preserved in the city museum at Pljevlje

J. Chr. Engel, Geschichte des Freistaates Ragusa, Wien 1809, p. 312, referring to the short notes of the ambassadors sent from Dubrovnik to the Turkish Pasha 1792; Pouqueville, Voyage de la Grèce, 1820, II, 470; Ami Boué, La Turque d' Europe I, 1840, 559, No.1; O. Blau, Monatsberichte der königlich preusischen Akademie der Wissenschaften zu Berlin, 1866 (1867) 847, No. 7; Patsch, WMBH IV, 281, No.18, with drawing; CIL III 8309(= 1708 = 6343); N. Vulić, Spomenik SKA 98, 1941-1948, No. 306, only the photo made by D. Segejevski. Cf. Hoernes, AEM 4, 1880, 188; G. Alföldy, Σπλαυνον – Splonum, Acta ant. hung. 10, 1-2, 1962, 3-12. in Beiträge zum Namenforschung 15, 1964, 98, n. 91 and idem, Bevölkerung und Gesellschaft der römischen Provinz Dalmatien, 1965, 58; J.J. Wilkes.

Σπλαυνυμ – Splonum again, Acta antiqua hung. 13, 1965, 11-124 and idem, Dalmatia 173

T. Aûr(elio) Sexûano |eq(uiti) R(omano)| dec(urioni) m(unicipii) S( ) T.Aûr(elius) Lu|percus filio | pientissimo|[5] in memoriam | posuit | l(ocus) d(atus) d(ecreto) d(ecurionum).

S( ) after M(*unicipium*) is interpreted as the abbreviated name of the city. It is completed in different ways in research today, either as the name of one of the forts known from the Roman wars in the Balkan countries at the beginning of the first century AD or as the name derived from that of the tribe settled in this region. Th. Mommsen, CIL III ad No. 8309 suggested, without discussing the problem, that *S* is to be understood as *Stanecli*, the station mentioned by Tabula Peutingeriana; A.J. Evans recognized the abbreviation for the *Municipium Splonum* in the letters M S in the inscription 1b as, the name deriving from the Splonistae tribe. This suggestion was accepted by N. Vulić, in Spomenik SKA 98, 130; however, in RE I A (1920) 2006 he admitted that the name of the city could be *Saloniana*.[55]

Splonum and *Municipium Splonistarum* are often quoted as the name of the Municipium at Pljevlja. There are two further inscriptions which deserve attention as being relevant in defining the name of the Roman municipium in Komini near Pljevlja. One of these is the inscription in which Evans recognized *Splonistae*. It was found in the village of Čadinje, not far from Prijepolje and lost today. Only the Evans copy has been preserved.

1b. Funerary monument in the form of a large square slab, with an inscribed field 35 cm in height and 35 cm in width (Hoernes). Found in the village of Čadinje on the bank of the river Lim, near Prijepolja. Lost.

M. Hoernes, AEM 4, 1880, 197, No 3b, following the copy made by the vice-consul of Austria at Pljevlja Müller; A. Evans, Antiquarian research, 1885, 44 with drawing, fig. 21; CIL III 8308, on the basis of the drawing given by vice-consul Müller to Hoernes. Cf G. Alföldy, Acta Ant. hung. 10, 1962, 4 ff. J.J. Wilkes, Acta antiqua hung. 13, 1965, 11-124 and idem, Dalmatia, 173.

D(is) M(anibus) s(acrum) | P.Ael(io) Pladome|[no] Carvañioni (?) an(norum) | [---praefecto)] civitaûum |[5] [---]M praef(ecto) | et d(ecurioni) mun(icipii) Aureli S[p]lo|n(istarum) | [et] Aęlia[e] Pantoñi con|[iu]gi eius viva(e) parenûbus | pientissimis ATEIL |[10] Titus, Lupus et Firmi|nus h(eredes) p(onendum) c(uraverunt) | h(ic) s(itus) e(st).

In lines 1-3 Domaszewski (in Hoernes, p. 197) recognized two names, Pladomenus and Carvanius, as cognomina of one and the same person, the latter signifying the place of origin. Evans, p. 45, completed the former in *Pladome[no]*, quoting inscriptions from Rider

---

[54] See A.J. Evans, Antiquarian researches 44; M. Mirković, Iz istorije Polimlja u rimsko doba, Godišnjak XIV, CBI 12, 1975, 95-108.

[55] A. Loma, in the article Zur Frage des Munizipiums S. und seines Namens, 185-230, Mélanges d'histoire et d'épigraphie offerts à Fanoula Papazoglou, collected different solutions, without offering any new.

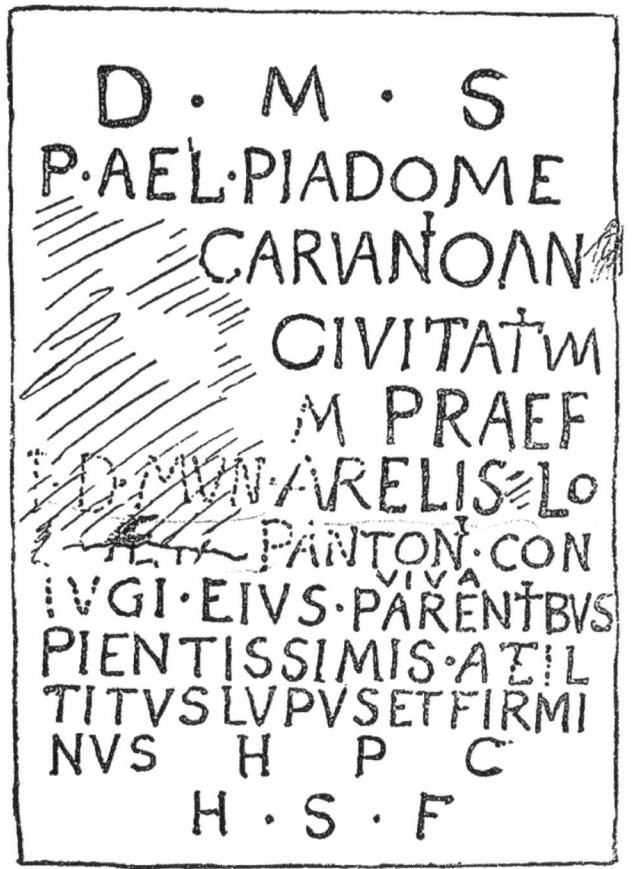

Fig. 22: Evans, Antiquarian researches, fig. 21

as attesting the same name, CIL III 2787 (*Pladomenus Sera Turi f.*), 2797 (*Vendo Tudania Pladomeni f.*), 6410 (*I.O.M. Aplv .dv//// Mevertens Pladomeni filius*); *Carvanio* closely resembles the name of the king Gentius' brother who appears in Livy as Caravantius. The name in line 3 could have the form –io, *Carvanio*, in Dativ Carvanioni. This reading is supported by the Evans drawing on which NI before O are in ligature, and the O is followed by two letters, probably NI; *[praefecto] civitatium* in line 4 is accepted by all. Evans adds *[Melco]m(anorum)* what should be the tribe quoting by Pliny in *conventus Naronitanus*, n.h..III 143. The completing *[Pirustaru]m* as well as *praefectus civitatium [Melcomanor]m* is as possible as any of the others, *[Arbensiu]m*, or *[Metlensiu]m* or *[Malvesatiu]m*, like in inscription No. **2** which follows. Line 7 is completed by Domaszewski in *[Aeliae Tes]toni* following the copy made by vice-consul Müller, in CIL III in *[et Aurel]ia[e] Pantoni*; Line 9: it is clear that *ATEIL* must be read as *Aelii*, signifying the common gentile of the three sons, Titus, Lupus and Firminus.

What is crucial for the debate about the name of the city near Pljevlja is the reading of line 6. In completing this line opinions differ greatly. Domaszewski (quoted by Hoernes) thought that it should be completed in *praefectus [iure dicundo municipii] Aurelii S(a)lo(niani)*. Saloniana is mentioned by Ptolemy among the inland cities of Dalmatia, far away from Pljevlja; for Evans a better reading would be *praefectus iure dicundo*

Municipii Aurelii S(p)lo(nistarum), which means the municipium of the mining community of the Splonistae. This completion is accepted by Wilkes, *Dalmatia*, 429, f. but G. Alföldy, Acta ant. hung. 10, 1962, and BNF 15, 1964, 98, nap. 91, completes the text in *[...praef.] civitatium [Pirustaru]m praef. [munic.] Aureli S[icu]lo(tarum)*.

Evans drawing, the only preserved document concerning this monument, seems to support the *praef(ectus) i(ure) d(icundo) mun(icipii) Aureli S[p]lo[nistarum]* reading. The letters I and D at the beginning of line 6, however uncertain, could be completed in *praefectus et d(ecurio) mun(icipii)*. The S which follows is certain on the drawing as reproduced in Evans's Antiquarian Research on p. 44, as well as LO after a small lacuna with a space for one letter. Evans's reading *S[p]lo[nistarum]* seems to be the most likely of all those suggested to date. It is supported by the fact that Splonistae appears once more in the inscription from Pljevlja, together with *Arbenses, Metlenses i Malvesatii*:

2. Altar made of limestone height 85, width 41, thick 35 cm. Found in the ruins of the Roman town and thereafter immured by Gavro Ostojić in his stable.

Sergejevski, GZM 52, 1940, 20, no. 4 with photo; Vulić, Spomenik 98, 1941-48, no. 287, with photo; (AE 1948, 242; A. et J. Šašel, ILJug., 1963, no. 73).

Serapidi | et Isidi M.| Ulp(ius) Gellia|nus eq(ues) R(omanus) |⁵ cur(ator) Arben|si(um) Metlensi(um) | Splonista(rum) | Maluensati(um).

Curatores were named by the emperor. It was their duty to regulate finances and taxes in the provinces. M. Ulpius Gellianus was responsible for four *civitates*. None of those *civitates* can be identified and localized for certain. It is suggested that *Arbenses* were the inhabitants of the island of Arba (Rab) in the Adriatic see, *Metlenses* took their name from the Japodian stronghold of *Metulum* and that *Malvesatii* gave its name to the municipium *Malvesatium* near present day Požega, in western Serbia.[56] *Splonistae* must derive from *Splonum*. It world be the second record of *Splonistae* in the same region, in Pljevlja or its surroundings.

The problem lies in the fact that there is no concrete evidence for the location of *Splonum*. Although it is mentioned in many inscriptions found in different places, none of them provide any useful information as to where the city was located. Splonum is mentioned in the inscription from Ampelum in Dacia, CIL III 1322 and in two another found in the region of Delmatae. In the inscription from Ampelum (CIL III 1322) there appears a *princeps adsignatus ex Splon(o)*. In the inscription from Salona CIL III 2026 a *curator rei publicae Splonistarum* is attested, who could not have been in charge of the place where the inscription was discovered. In the

---

[56] Sergejevki and Vulić; Cf. Wilkes, Dalmatia, 283 f. On municipijum Malvesatium near Visibaba to-day see F. Papazoglou, Le municipium Malvesatium et son territoire, Živa Antika 7, 1957, 113-122.

inscription from Sućurac near Split, CIL III 8783 *q(uinquennalis?) municip. Pasinatium Splonistarum Arupinorum* is mentioned. The place where these inscriptions were discovered fails to indicate the position of Splonistae or of the municipium Splonum. The name appears not alone, but usually together with others *civitates* or cities. Splonum is mentioned by Cassius Dio LVI 11,1.2, as a stronghold surrounded by the Romans and captured in AD 9 together with Raetinium and Seretion. It is suggested that Raetinium was not far from present day Bihać; the position of Seretion and Splonum is unknown.

The discussion about Splonum and its position was renewed by G. Alföldy in 1962 and J.J. Wilkes in 1965 in papers concerning the location of the fort. It is mentioned by Dio Cassius and Velleius Paterculus in describing the events of the revolt in Dalmatia and Pannonia in AD 8 and 9. Despite using the same evidence, that given by Cassius Dio and Velleius, they differ strongly in their conclusions. In Alföldy's opinion the data about the Roman action against the rebels in the years 8 and 9 may not rectify Evans's location of Splonum so far in the south, in the North of present day Montenegro.[57] Roman troops marched from the Sava valley and the additional information preserved in Dio's work suggests that they took the direction towards central Bosnia to meet the rebels in the fort at Splonum. Therefore he believes that Splonum might have been located in the vicinity of present day Šipovo, in the Piva valley, not far from Jajce in Bosnia. The data about Splonum, in his opinion, cannot contribute to solving the problem of the name of the Municipium nearby Pljevlja.

According to Alföldy another explanation must be found for the abbreviation S in the inscription from Pljevlja. He links it with the name *Siculotae* which would designate one of the *civitates peregrinae* in the region of Pljevlja and Prijepolje. *Siculi* are to be recognized in the inscription from Čadinja. He completes the damaged text in *Municipium S[icu]lo(tarum)*.[58] They would be the people which was transported from the region between Salona and Tragurion to the region of present day northern Montenegro in the deserted zone after the Roman conquest in AD 9. Pirustae who inhabited this region were in his opinion destroyed in the war with the Romans and transported to work in the mines in Dacia.

J.J. Wilkes admits that there was a large Roman settlement near Šipovo in the Pliva valley, but its identification with Splonum, the Illyrian stronghold captured in 9 and later known as municipium Splonistarum, is in his opinion not supported by evidence.[59] On the other hand he sees no obstacle for the location of Splonum in northern Montenegro near Pljevlja, even in the description of the events regarding the movement of the Roman army against the rebels in Dalmatia by Cassius Dio and Velleius. Starting from the same evidence as G. Alföldy, from the data in Cassius Dio and Velleius concerning the actions of Tiberius and Germanicus in the years 8 and 9, he discusses the possibility of reaching northern Montenegro in a march from the Sava valley. It is his opinion that in these years the Roman strength may have pacified the most part of the interior of Illyricum, which means that they had enough time to reach northern Montenegro starting from the Sava valley. If located near Pljevlja, Splonum could have been on the route the Romans followed when fighting against the rebel tribes in Dalmatia.

The crucial argument which could help to resolve the completion of the abbreviation S is still missing There is still a choice between two hypothesis: to accept Evans's proposal to locate Splonum in the vicinity of Pljevlja and recognize it in the abbreviation S. or to seek a new solution in connecting S. with the newcomers, the Siculi from the coastal region in Dalmatia. However, the mention of Splonistae in the inscriptions from Pljevlja and its surroundings speaks more in favour of the hypothesis that Municipium S. was a municipium Splonistarum. The name of Municipium S could be connected with Splonum and Splonistae in a different way. Splonum could have been located in the region of Pljevlja, but the original position of Splonistae might not necessarily have been located here.

b) CITY ADMINISTRATION

The name of the municipim remains an enigma. Nevertheless, there is no doubt that it was a municipal settlement as shown by the inscriptions of city chancellors, *duoviri, decuriones, quinquennales*. New excavations show that it was a large and prosperous city with two big cemeteries containing hundreds of graves. To *Genio Municipii* and the *Deae Xantae Nemesi* (no. **11**).

The Municipium was administered, as other cities in the Empire, *by duoviri* and *decuriones*, among them *quienquaennales* and *aediles*. The city chancellors as *ordo decurionum* decided about what happened on the city territory, as erection of the monuments, building temple and similar.

Duovirs are known from the following altars:

3. Altar of limestone, found in Pljevlja; Patsch saw it in front of the mosque Čutkovac. Disappeared.

Patsch, WMBH IV, 1896, 279, no. 10; CIL III 8304; N. Vulić, Spomenik 98, 1941-48, 134, no. 295, with phot. by D. Sergejevski.

I(ovi) O(ptimo) M(aximo) f(ulguratori) | *M. Aemil(ius)* | *Ântonius* | *II vir* | *l(ibens) p(osuit)*.

M. Aemilius Antonius appears again in on the funeral monument of Aemilius Calvinus who died in Salona.

---
[57] G. Alföldy, Σπλαυνον – Splonum, Acta ant. hung. 10, 1-2, 1962, 3-12. and idem, BNF 15, 1964, 98, n. 91 and idem, Bevölkerung und Gesellschaft der römischen Provinz Dalmatien, 1965, 58.
[58] G. Alföldy, 58
[59] Σπλαυνον – Splonum again, Acta antiqua hung. 13, 1965, 11-124. Cf idem, Dalmatia 173.

City duovir Aemilius Titianus belonged the same family:

4. Altar of limestone, found on the hill Ilijino Brdo, in the church, on the left of the church altar, with the text on the side interred in the ground (Sergejevski).

Blau, Acta Acad. Berol. 1866, 847; Hoernes, AEM IV, 1880, 187; Patsch, WMBH IV, 1896, 285, no. 26, with drawing; CIL III 8301 (6341) + p....; Sergejevski, Spomenik 98, 1941-48, 145, with drawing.

I(ovi) O(ptimo) M(aximo) | M. Aemil(ius) Ti|tianus II vi(r) | q(uin)q(ennalis) l(ibens) p(osuit).

Line 2: MA.MIL. CIL III 8341, AEMIL Blau, CIL III 6341, Hoernes: M. Âemil Patsch, Sergejevski.

Decurio was one of *Paconii*, from one of the leading families in the city.

5. Funerary cipus of limestone with blue lines, height 163, width 72, thick 22 cm. Inscribed field in the frame decorated as the 'fish-bone'. Discovered during the excavation of the Necropolis II, in 1967, in one of the graves in the tomb II at Komini, in a room with the ashes box.

A. Cermanović-Kuzmanović, Hommage à Marcel Renard III, 1969, 118 with phot. and eadem, Starinar 18, 1967, 202, no. 1, with phot. (A. et J. Šašel, ILJug. 611).

D(is) M(anibus) s(acrum) | L. P(aconio) Barbaro | d(ecurioni) m(unicipii) ? R. q(ui) v̂i(xit) ânni(s) | X̂X m(ensibus) III d(iebus) IIII L.P(aconius) Barbar( ) | et Aur(elia) Panto | filio incon|parabili et | sibi vivi in | felicisimi (!) | p(osuerunt).

In line 3 the O is on engraved on the frame; smaller letter BARO in line 2 and ANNI at the end of the line 3, ON at the end of l. 8.

The letter *R* after *m(unicipii)* gives ground for discussion. If connected with *municipium* the *R* could be abbreviated name of the a city. That means Paconius was not a *decurio* in the city where he was buried. This interpretation is, however, not the only possible. The *R* could be a part of the nomenclature formula of Paconius. He could be *L. Paconius Barbarus R*. This letter could have the same function as G in the wife's name and R in the name of the daughter in the same family on the monument found in the another tomb on the same cemetery, No.75.

Decurio was also Aurelius Maximus Argenianus:

6. Funerary cipus of limestone height 141, width 82, thick 63 cm. The inscribed field in the floral frame. On the right lateral side man's figure in the profiled field wearing a short cloth and the Frigian cape on his head and a short hiton. Similar figure on the left lateral side. The human figure wears the three-corner hut on his head. The frame on both lateral sides decorated with wine and 'fish-bone'. Discovered on the Necropolis II, during the excavations in 1966, in the separated room in the tomb I.

A. Cermanović-Kuzmanović, Hommage à Marcel Renard III, 1969, 118 with photo and eadem, Starinar 18, 1967, 203, no. 3, with photo (A. et J. Šašel, ILJug. 6049). Cf. Cermanović-Kuzmanović, Materijali IV, 7, Kongres arheologa Jugoslavije, Herzeg Novi 1966, 82, with photo Cf. D. Srejović, Zbornik Narodnog Muzeja Beograd VIII, 1975, 181 f.

D(is) M(anibus) S(acrum) | Aur(elius) Ma|ximus | Argeni|anus d(ecurio) m(unicipii) | v(ivus) s(ibi) p(osuit) et Âûr̂(eliae) | Maximîn̂ê (!)| filie(!) que (!) v̂(ixit) ân(nos) XXX.

7. Fragment of the funerary monument, upper part height 95, width 57, thick 23 cm. In vaulted aedicule were engraved three portraits of which are preserved one representing the male and one female on the right side. Angles on the outside of the arch decorated by roses and the acanthus leaves. Above aedicule is represented gable in relief and the stylized leaves in the corners. Discovered during the archaeological investigations 1965 in the Necropolis II.

A. Cermanović-Kuzmanović, Zbornik Filozofskog fakulteta XI-1, 1970, 79 f., no.6 with phot. 6.

[D(is) M(anibus)] s(acrum)] [   ] io St|[   ]io d(ecurioni) m(unicipii) | [   ]ius [

8. Limestone slab height 50, width 77, thick 61 cm. Discovered in the minaret of the Podstražica mosque.

Blau, Acta acad. Berol. 1866, 847 (CIL III 6344); Hoernes, AEM 4, 1888, 187; CIL III 8310; Patsch, GZM 6, 1894, 471 and idem, WMBH 4, 1896, 279, no. 11, with drawing, fig. 8; N. Vulić, Spomenik 98, 1941-48, 136, no. 300 with photo.

*[   ] q(uin)q(uennali) et sacerd[oti] | [et...... sac]erdotali et Au[r(elio? | [   ]um P.Ael(lii) Firmini [ ].
P.Ael(io) Firmino ??] q(uin)q(uennali) et sacerd[oti prov(inciae) et Au[reliae? Max]um(ae) P.Ael(ius) Firmini[anus...* Patsch.

9. Limestone slab height 31, width 60 cm. It was in the yard of the Husein-pasha mosque at Pljevlja in the time when N. Vulić saw it.

Blau, Acta acad. Berol. 1866, 848 (CIL III 6345); Hoernes, AEM 4, 1880, 187; Patsch, GMBH 6, 1894, 473 and idem, WMBH 4, 1896, 281, 14, with drawing CIL III 8311; N. Vulić, Spomenik 98, 1941-48, 136, no. 299, with photo.

[   ] et epulo dedi|cavit | l(oco) d(ato) d(ecreto) d(ecurionum)

An altar was erected in honor of the emperor on Ilijino Brdo hill, as the *ordo decurionum* decided, no. **18**. See also the inscription from Sveta Trojica, no. **42**).

As in others cities in the Balkan provinces the people holding the municipal offices in the Roman municipium in Komini near Pljevlja, *duoviri* and *decuriones*, were Roman citizens. To this class belonged *Aemilii* or *Paconii*. It might be supposed that *Aurelii* among the decurions, like Aurelius Maximus Argenianus (**6**), originated from native families, who got the Roman citizenship from Marcus Aurelius or even later, under Caracalla. Interesting is the case of Paconius (**5**) whose wife Aurelia Panto must have originate from the Illyrian family.

c) THE ORIGIN OF THE ROMAN CITY

It is not possible to establish beyond any doubt when and how the municipium sprung up. The beginning of the settlement and the municipal organization are not necessarily contemporary. They are probably not to be dated in the same time. One or another could be approximately dated, the former at the end of the first century BC, the later not before the second century AD. Finding an answer to the question as to how the settlement sprung up in this place is more complicated.

Archaeological investigations which were carried out between 1965 and 1967 and again from 1970 to 1972 have shown that the burials in the older part of the necropolis, the so called necropolis I, began at the end of the first century BC.; they were continued in necropolis II in the first century and later, also sporadically, in the fourth century. Both necropoli were in use until the fourth century. In the first three centuries the incineration was practiced. The type of graves changed in the 4th century, with skeletons being buried in the old tombs. That means that the settlement existed here continuously from the last half of the first century BC until Late Antiquity, but that new people came to live here in the fourth century. Indications about the beginning of the municipium could not be found in the inscriptions. One or two belong probably to the 1st century. As far as they can be approximately dated, they mostly belong to the time from the second half of the 2nd century to the middle of the 3th. The oldest dated inscription found in the municipium belongs to the time of the reign of Antoninus Pius, and can be dated to the years 138 and 161:

10. Upper part of the limestone base: height 53, width 49, thick 38 cm. Letters 5.5 to 2.5 cm. Found in the ruins of Velika džamija (the Great Mosque) in 1940.

Sergejevski, GZM 53, 1941; N. Vulić, Spomenik 98, 1941-48, no. 298 with photo. (A. et J. Šašel, ILJug, 71).

> *[L.Ael]io Aure\[lio C]ommodo | [Imp.T.] Aeli Caes(aris) p(atris) | [Ant]onini Aug(usti) |⁵ [f(ilio) divi] Hadri\[ani n(epoti)]*
> Lines 3-4: *[imp.T.] Aeli Caes(aris) p(atri) | [p(atriae)* Sergejevski, *imp.T.] Ael. Caes(aris) p.,* Vulić; *[co(n)s(uli) L.] Aeli Caes(aris) p(atris)* Šašel, Lines 5-6: *[Pii] Hadri\[ani f(ilio) divi Tra]\[iani* Sergejevski. *[f(ilio) divi] Hadri\[ani n(epoti)* Vulić, *[Pii fil(io) divi Hadri\ani] n(epoti)* Šašel.

The altar was dedicated to Lucius Aelius Aurelius Commodus, the son of Lucius Aelius Caesar and can be dated to the year 138 rather than to the years 154-161, when he shared the throne with the emperor Marcus (Šašel).

The name Aurelius, which prevailed in other monuments, points to the connection with the emperor Marcus, after the 60s of the second century or later with Caracalla who granted Roman citizenship to all free inhabitants of the Empire in 212. *Aurelii* on the monuments from the municipium in Komini could refer to new citizens, from the time the settlement was granted municipal status.

It could not be established with certainty either when or how the municipium in Komini near Pljevlja arose. Different ways could lead to the foundation of the Roman town in the provinces: the municipium could have originated from the native community which developed in the city under Roman rule and was granted the status of Roman city; a municipium often grew from the community of Roman citizens who lived in the native surroundings, usually on the main roads, as *conventus civium Romanorum*; many municipia developed near the military camps or in the mining regions, in the first case with their nucleus as the agglomeration initially inhabited by merchants and their families, and thereafter the soldiers' families and veterans. Mining personnel with their families and immigrants from other provinces lived in the municipal settlements near the mines. The most of this possibility could be hardly proved in Komini. No military unit was garrisoned at Pljevlja or in its surroundings; Roman mines have not yet been discovered there; and there is no reason to suppose the existence of a large merchant community, because the place was not crossed by any important road. However, the presence of a great number of Illyrian natives and of soldiers who presumably served in the auxiliary units has made it necessary to discuss two of these possibilities: the development of a Roman town at the location of the native settlement or from the settlement of ex- soldiers.

Natives, pre-Roman settlement and the municipium

In his study Le droit Latin et les cités romaines sous l'Empire, Ch. Saumagne argues that there is no known example which allows the hypothesis that the meaning of the word municipium lies in a community of Roman citizens. He grounded his opinion on the large epigraphic evidence from North Africa.[60] The great number of native names in the inscriptions from Komini and Pljevlja seems to speak in favour of the thesis that it was not originally here a community of Roman citizens. The Illyrian names as the only name, without *gentile* in the city and in the surroundings, show that the local natives also survived under Roman rule or were transported here from the Roman authority. Furthermore, the names doubtlessly prove the presence of a large number of natives in the city and its territory. They appear in the inscriptions as the

---
[60] Ch. Saumagne, Le droit Latin et les cites romaines sous l'Empire, Sirey 1965.

predominant component in the city. However, it is difficult to prove that it was a native settlement which was granted the status of Roman municipium from the emperor. There is no archaeological evidence to prove the existence of a native settlement in pre-Roman times in Komini or anywhere in the Ćehotina valley. The archaeological material collected to date in the Lim and Ćehotina valley and in necropolis I and II in Komini does not prove that the region was inhabited in the centuries preceding the Roman conquest, i.e. between the 6th and the 2nd century BC. All excavations carried out until now in the surroundings of Pljevlje, like in tumulus at Otilovići[61] show the same picture: there are no grave goods or burial types which could be dated between the end of the Bronze age and the arrival of the Romans. No tumulus point to a post Bronze Age culture. The only finding which could weaken this conclusion is the tumulus in Krajčinovici with Celtic material which also allows us to suppose the presence of people from the La Tène civilization in this region. However, this locality is about 35 km from Komini.

The lack of archaeological discoveries which can be dated between the end of the Bronze age and the La Tène culture or the beginning of the Roman settlement could be accidental. Future explorations in the vicinity of Komini, on Ilijino Brdo and in Plijes in the middle of the valley where the municipium arose could change this picture. It could be assumed that a Pre-Roman settlement existed somewhere in the Ćehotina valley, on Ilijino Brdo, where Arthur Evans discovered remains of the prehistoric, in his opinion Bronze-age culture, on the slope of the hill. The absence of archaeological material in the city necropolis I and II earlier than the second half of the first century BC is more significant. It is evident that there is no prehistoric settlement at this location.

Further difficulty in the debate about the city's origins arose from the interpretation of the nomenclature in the inscriptions. Only a few examples could be linked with the pre-Roman stratum in the region. The Illyrian names in the inscriptions found in Komini and Pljevlja, and in their surroundings as well as in Kolovrat near Prijepoje have corresponding parallels in the onomastic of Dalmatia. They could belong to the specific large group of peoples living in the middle Illyrian region that stretches from the Adriatic to the Ibar valley. The similarity with the Dalmatian onomastic suggests however the possibility of the future inhabitants of the municipium in Komini emigrating from the region of Dalmatia or being transported to live here in the non-inhabited area in the Lim and Ćehotina valley. The strong similarity with the nomenclature in the coastal zone in Dalmatia could have meant that many of the inhabitants of the municipium originated from these regions, not far from Rider, Vrlika and Salona. The transportation of subject peoples from one country to another was a well known practice in the Roman world. The best known example is the transportation of the Pirustae tribe to Dacia, to serve in the Roman mines. Although the removal of people from the coastal zone, or from the land belonging to Siculi seems to be likely, direct evidence is lacking. Nevertheless, the majority of names in the municipium in Komini appear in inscriptions from the Adriatic cost to the Ibar river valley; on the other hand, there are names in the municipium which are unique or very rare in the rest of the Illyrian world. They might belong to the original, pre-Roman inhabitants in the region between the rivers Lim and Ćehotina. If so, we have to counter two unequal groups of natives, one smaller in number belonging to the rest of the people once living in this region and another transported here in Roman times from the region of Rider and Vrlike originally inhabited by the Delmatae. The portraits on the monument from the Ćehotina and Lim valley show characteristics of two different races.[62] It has been suggested that the Romans transported the natives to the Ćehotina valley from the region of Siculi, not far from Salona[63] in order to procure land for the Roman veterans. This conclusion is based on the interpretation and reconstruction of inscription no. 1b in *municipium Siculotarum*. The natives in the Municipium in Komini or on its territory could belong to two branches, one belonging to the rest of the pre-Roman people in this region, probably few in number, and one which migrated under the Romans from the coastal zone.

There is no evidence to indicate the existence of a pre-Roman settlement prior to the Roman municipium or to confirm that the native settlement was granted the status of a Roman city, but there are grounds to believe that people of Illyrian origin lived there and contributed greatly to the growth of the Roman town. The old population which survived the Roman occupation was not numerous. They lived under the Romans as country dwellers on the *ager publicus* and paid taxes as peregrini. The second important element in making the Roman city were presumably former soldiers, not from the legions, but from the auxiliary units.

Soldiers and ex-soldiers in the municipium

It is well known fact that legions and their soldiers played an important role in the urbanization of the Roman provinces in the Balkans. Military camps, not only those of the legions, but also of the auxiliary troops, were the point which attracted merchants and their families to settle in their vicinity; soldiers joined them upon completion of their military service. Legionary veterans were often rewarded with land and were colonized by the State in the provinces far from their forts.[64] However legionary veterans played no role in the Roman municipium near Pljevlja. There was no important military base in Komini, nor were there a great number of soldiers in service here, as it was in the legionary forts in

---

[61] Information from M. Ružic who carried out excavations on this location near Pljevlje in 2009.

[62] A. Cermanović-Kuzmanović, Die Römische-illyrischen Skulpturen aus Komini, Antike Welt 2, 1973, 6-7.

[63] G. Alföldy, Bevölkerung, 57-58.

[64] S. Ferjančić, Naseljavanje legijskih veterana u Balkanskim provincijama, I-III vek n.e., Belgrade 2002.

Burnum or in Bigeste near Narona in western Dalmatia. There are no grounds to suppose that the colonization of the legionary veterans was carried out in Komini. Only a few legionary soldiers are recorded in the inscriptions from Pljevlja. They have no connction with the origin with the municipium. They served here mostly as *beneficiarii*.

1. The beneficiarii post

The post of *beneficiarii* was situated in the city territory, manned by the soldiers from the Dalmatian and Pannonian legions who served their one or two year duty here controlling traffic, customs and the local population. Some of them appear on the monument found in Komini or on Ilijino Brdo or in Pljevlje. They probably left the altars at the end of their service Flavius Saturninus served in the legion XI Claudia:

11. Limestone altar: height 84, width 43, thick 38.5 cm. Decorated with a rosette on the top, and an ornamental base. It was immured in the stable of Gavro Ostojic in Komini.

Vulić, Spomenik XCIII, 1940-1948, no. 24; A. Cermanović-Kuzmanović, Starinar 20, 1969, 25, with photo (A. et J. Šašel, ILJug. 602).

> *Deae Xante (!) | Nemesi et geni|o Municipi Fl(avius) | Saturninus* ⁵*| b{b}(ene)f(iciarius) co(n)s(ularis) | leg(ionis) XI Cl(audiae) | libies (!) posuit.*

Line 3: Fl(avius) Vulić, h(uius) Cerm.-Kuzm.

Xante insetad of *sanctae*.

Beneficiarius P. Aelius Fuscinus served in the pannonian I Adiutrix legion:

12. Limestone altar: height 80, width 41, thick 20 cm. It was immured in the Mustafa beg Selmanovic's house in Pljevlje.

Patsch, GMBH 6, 1894, 475, no. 23 and WMBH IV, 1896, 282, no. 23, with drawing fig. 15; CIL III 13847.

> *I(ovi) O(ptimo) M(aximo) s(acrum) | P. Ael(ius) Fusci|nus mil(es) leg(ionis) | I Ad(iutricis) b̂(ene)f(iciarius) co(n)s(ularis) | Im̂p(eratore) L. Sep̂t(imio) Sevêro | Pert(inace) Âug(usto) êt Al̂bi(no) Caes(are) | co(n)s(ulibus) v(otum) l(ibens) m(erito) p(osuit).*

The emperor Septimius Severus and Albinus Caesar were consules together in the year 194.

Two beneficiarii consularis were buried in necropoluis II in Komini:

13. Limestone funerary monument: height 156 width 74, thick 30 cm. In the triangular gable above the inscribed field there is a wreath with leaves and flowers. Letters 5 cm in height. Discovered above the grave with the arches in cemetery II in Komini 1965.

A. Cermanović-Kuzmanović, Starinar 18, 1967, 204 no. 4, with photo. and eadem, Hommage à Marcel Renard, Coll. Latomus 103, 118-119, with phot. (A. et J. Šašel, ILJug. 607).

> *D(is) M(anibus) s(acrum) | Aulo Gab̂i|lio Liberali | q(ui) v(ixit) a(nnis) XXIIX | Fl(avius) Aper | b(ene)f(iciarius) co(n)s(ularis) m(emoriam) p(osuit).*

Lines 2-3: *Gab|lio* Cerm.-Kuzm. It seems that the letter *I* is inscribed above the B in GABL

Another *beneficiarius* lived in Komini with his family. His wife bears the Illyrian name Apla:

14. Funerary monument of crumbly limestone, height 120, width 57, thick 30 cm. broken in two parts The upper right part is missing The inscription is damaged. Discovered in necropolis II in 1965.

A. Cermanović-Kuzmanović, Zbornik Filozofskog fakulteta Beograd XI-1, 1970, 78, no.4 with phot. (A. et J. Šašel, ILJug. 617).

> *D(is) M(anibus) S(acrum) | Apla [ ] |Aur( ) Is[ ] | DET [ ]|io b(ene)f(iciarius)? [an]||nos (?) XX[ ] | piis( ).*

Apla is an Illyrian name (see below, p. 46).

None of the cited monuments can be connected with a permanent garrison at this location or with the origin of the city. The province of Dalmatia has two legionary garrisons until the time of Domitian.[65] Thereafter, at the time when the province of Dalmatia had no legionary garrison, *beneficiarii* were taken from the Pannonian legions. They stayed in the same place for one or two years at the most.[66] The earliest monument among them, no. 11, was that of the soldier of the *XI Claudia* legion who was sent to the post in Komini while the legion was still garrisoned at Burnum in Dalmatia. It left the Dalmatian camp in 68 and never returned. At first it was transported to Upper Germania province and thereafter, under Trajan, to Durostorum on the lower Danube, where it spent the subsequent centuries.[67] It is highly unlikely that the *beneficiarius* mentioned on the monument from Komini was transported from the *XI Claudia* legion to be beneficiarius in the region of Pljevlja after 68, when the legion was far away from Dalmatia. If so, we must assume that the station of the *beneficiarii* was situated in Komini before Vespasian came to power, at the end of the 60s of the first century. The station was still in the

---

[65] On Roman army in Dalmatia see J.J. Wilkes, Dalmatia, London 1969, 88-152.

[66] About this military charge see M. Mirković, Beneficiarii consularis in Sirmium. Inschriften, *Chiron* 24, 1994, 346-404.

[67] Ritterling, Legio, 1698; Patsch, Der Kampf um den Donauraum unter Domitian und Trajan, Beiträge zur Völkerkunde von Südosteuropa, 1937, 3, n. 4.

same place in the second half of the second or in the early third century. The name *Aurelius* belonging to the *beneficiarius* on monument no. **14** allows us to date it after the emperor Marcus. He probably married a woman from the village near the stationo. Her name Apla is Illyrian. The presence of *beneficiarii* at this spot is attested in the year 194 (no. 12) when the soldier from the Pannonian legion *I Adiutrix* was in service here. This legion sent *beneficiarii* all over the province of Dalmatia, to Salona, Burnum, Doclea and present day Ljubuško.[68]

The beneficiary post in the municipium was presumably situated near one of the city gates with a staff of no more than ten *beneficiarii*. Another one could be expected on Ilijino Brdo. None have been discovered to date. The duty of *beneficiarii* was at first to control tax collection, then to police the region.[69] It seems likely that some of them married the local women and stayed in this region permanently upon completion of their military service.

The legionary soldiers appear on the monument from this region not only as *beneficiarii*. A twenty three year old soldier from the *XIII Gemina, Âe(ius) Felicia|nus* was interred on Ilijino Brdo (no. **35**). He probably originated from this region. His parents took care of his burial, *filio| dul(cissimo) Maxi|mus êt Fi|aêtia p(arentes)*. He could have been recruited relatively early, if we take into consideration the fact that the *XIII Gemina* was garrisoned in Illyricum in the first century, from the time of the Dalmatian and Pannonian revolt. In 69-70 it was still in Poetovio, and after 103 in Vindobona, far north: Trajan transported it to Dacia. The soldier Aelius Felicianus might have been recruited in the first century, before the legion left for Dacia. After dying in his twenty fifth year he was buried in his birth place.

2. Soldiers and veterans of auxiliary units in the city and on the city territory

The auxiliary veterans could also be granted land, as attested by the military diplomas CIL XVI 25 or be allowed to settle on the *ager publicus* mostly individually but also as a group on the land in special areas, as proved by the concentration of military diplomas or the inscriptions found in Banasa and Volubilis, on the territory of Viminacium and in some places in Dalmatia.[70] Some auxiliary soldiers are recorded in the municipium.

A centurion of the *cohors II Delmatarum* appears as the husband of Ratonia Autumna who was buried in the municipal necropolis II in Komini:

15. Limestone funerary monument broken into many fragments, four of which have been preserved. Total dimensions: height 108, width 75, thick 35 cm. A wreath on the upper part in the triangular frame, with a rosette in the middle. Discovered in necropolis II in Komini.

A. Cermanović-Kuzmanović, Hommage à Marcel Renard III, 1969, 118 with photo Taf. XL, Abb.2 (A. et J. Šašel, ILJug. 612)

[D(is)] M(anibus) S(acrum) | Ratoñiâe Âu|tumnâe q(uae) v(ixit) | ân(nis) XL Scard( ) | Asidoñius | Viêllianu|s (centurio) côh(ortis) II mil(iariae) | c(oniugi) c(arissimae) p(osuit).

Cohors II miliaria is probably *Cohors II miliaria Delmatarum* (Cermanović)[71] which was founded in 170, together with the *I miliaria Delmatarum* and recruited from within Dalmatia, mostly among natives. It has been assumed that the permanent camp of this unit was near Čačak in present day western Serbia. The soldiers of the cohors appear in the inscriptions in Salona, Dubrava and Čačak.[72] Asidonius Vitelianus, with a rare gentile name,[73] does not present himself as a veteran; he seems not to have been in service any more because he was married and his wife was no longer young (forty years old). He could be the former *centurio* of the cohort who settled in the municipium. There is no reason to assume the presence of the cohors at this location, because no other monuments indicate that it was garrisoned anywhere in the Lim valley or to suppose that he originated from this region where both names, Asidonius and Vitelianus, were unknown. With the name Ratonia, which is unique in the western provinces of the Empire,[74] his wife originated from Scardona in Dalmatia as is indicated in her funerary inscription. This means that Asidonius Vitellianus and his wife were both strangers in this region and were settled in the municipium. It could be assumed that he was given land on the city territory as a former soldier or that as a former auxiliary soldier he was allowed to settle on the *ager publicus* near the city.

It might be assumed that another two soldiers served in the auxiliary units:

16. Limestone funerary monument; height 150, width 83, thick 29 cm. In the upper part of the monument there is a wreath in the triangle frame with a rosette in the middle and branches and leaves have been engraved in the corners. Discovered in necropolis II *in situ*, near the grave with the incinerated dead.

A. Cermanović-Kuzmanović, Starinar 18, 1967, 204, no. 5, with phot. and eadem, Hommage à Marcel Renard III, 1969, 119, with photo (A. et J. Šašel, ILJug. 603).

D(is) M(anibus) S(acrum) | T. Aurel(ius) Apliñi | vetr(ano) (!) q(ui) v(ixit) a(nnis) LXX | êt Aûr(eliae)

---

[68] A. et J. Šašel, ILJug. 832 i 2808 (Burnum), 1825 (Doclea), 2086 Salona, 1919 (Ljubuški).
[69] M. Mirković, Beneficiarii consularis in Sirmium, Chiron 24, 1994, 348 i d. The post of befeficiarii in Sirmium was situated by the western city gate.
[70] M. Mirković, Military diplomas from Viminacium and the settlement of auxiliary veterans: city or countryside? Kaiser, Heer und Gesellschaft in der Römischen Kaiserzeit, Gedenkschrift für Eric Birley, 2000, 365-375.
[71] Less probably *cohors II nova miliaria equitata c. R.* (Šašel) which was not garrisoned in Dalmatia.
[72] G. Alföldy, Die Auxiliartruppen der Provinz Dalmatien, Mavors Roman Army Researches, III, 1987, 252.
[73] The name Asidonius is attested in Dalmatia and in Spain (Lörincz, Onomasticon s.v.).
[74] Lörincz, Onomasticon s.v. in this example.

V̂endoñi | coniûgi T.Âûr(elius) Turus p(arentibus) p(iissimis) p(osuit).

With a native name as his patronymic and his wife and son also bearing native names, it seems highly unlikely that Aurelius Aplini (filius) served in the Roman legion. He probably acquired the name Aurelius together with Roman citizenship after completing his military service in an ala or in the cohorts. The names of his father – *Aplis*, his wife – *Vendo* and his son – *Turus*, all belong to the Illyrian nomenclature. He was also granted *ius conubii* with his peregrine wife at the same time, after twenty five years of military service, *et conubium cum uxoribus*, as was formulated in military diplomas.[75] His son could have lawfully inherited him. His name *Aureius*, the same as that of the emperor Marcus, shows that he could have been discharged and granted *civitas* in the 60s-80s of the second century. That means that he was enrolled in the middle of this century, perhaps as a native of this region.

Non-Roman origin is also to be supposed for Aurelius Maximus whose mother was Illyrian *Vendo*:

17. Limestone funerary monument. In the upper part two portraits are represented under the vault, a woman with a scarf on her head and a man with an indefinable object in front of him. There is an inscribed field in the profiled frame. Found in Komini and transported to Pljevlja, where it was seen in the yard of the house belonging to Abdul effendi Karahmetović.

Vulić, Spomenik LXXI, 1931, no. 285 to the copy and photo made by Čed. Potparić, employer in Pljevlja, and Spomenik 98, 1941-48, 291 with photo made by D. Sergejevski.

D(is) M(anibus) s(acrum) | Âûr̂(elia) V̂eñdo | s(ibi) viva p(osuit) | êt Âûr̂(elio) Ma|ximo m̂i|liti filio | q(ui) (vixit) ân(nis) XXV.

The buried man could have been a *miles* in an auxiliary unit rather than in a legion because he was Illyrian by birth, as is clearly shown by his mother's name *Vendo*. The name Aurelius provides us with the grounds to date the monument in the second half of the second or in the first half of the third century.

All three inscriptions of the soldiers and veterans from Komini and Pljevlja, including that of the auxiliary centurion belong to the period after the emperor Marcus Aurelius. They might indicate a settlement of auxiliary veterans at this location. The colonization was presumably not organized as *deductio* by the state, but rather was allowed by the state or city authority in order to strengthen the existing community in which the Romanized immigrants and natives from the coastal zone of the province represented the majority. There is no known colony of veterans from auxiliary units which was organized by the emperor, neither were the former soldiers of alae and cohortes numerous in the Roman colonies.[76] The former auxiliary soldiers could represent the second colonization in the city and its territory. The first preceded over it for one or one and a half centuries and probably consisted of natives from the territory of Dalmatia. The quoted inscriptions in Pljevlja and Komini represent only indirect evidence about the colonization of the former auxiliary soldiers in the Roman city near Pljevlja. The hypothesis about the possible individual settlement of auxiliary veterans in this region, based on the few data, could be supported by further, also indirect arguments.

The individual settlement of auxiliary veterans in great numbers in the same place, especially on the city territory, could be assumed in many places in the provinces, in Volubilis and Banasa in northern Africa, and in Viminacium in Upper Moesia.[77] They also stayed on to live with their families near their military camp, as for instance in Timacum Minus in Upper Moesia. It could be assumed that in all these cases the State directed the individual settlement on the *ager publicus* where land was available. Auxiliary soldiers could be granted land allotments, as recorded in the military diploma CIL XVI 25 from AD 79 and together with this they were exempted from the payment of taxes.[78] There are cases where the city authorities allowed the settlement of veterans. A well known example is recorded in an inscription from Humac, on the city territory of Narona in the province of Dalmatia: *Divo Augusto et Ti. Casari Aug. f. Sacrum veterani pagi Scunastic(i) quibus colonia Naronit(ana) agros dedit.*[79] A great number of inscriptions not only of the veterans of the *VII Claudia* legion, but also of soldiers who served in the *III Alpinorum* or *I Belgarum* cohorts and others have been discovered in this region, in Humac and Ljubuško.[80] The city authority disposed of the large territory were the veterans could be settled.

The large number of Illyrian and other native names in the families of many *Aurelii* in the municipium, primarily of women, speaks in favour of the hypothesis that they many of them received Roman rights and the right to marry peregrine women, e.g. to have *conubium* with them by emperors' rescript, probably as former soldiers of the auxiliary troops after serving 25 years or more.

---

[75] On the privileges enjoyed by Roman auxiliary soldiers see S. Linke, Konzepte der Privilegierung römischer Veteranen, Stuttgart 1989, 7-15.

[76] For Scupi in Moesia Superior, for example, only two former auxiliary soldiers are recorded, cf. B. Josifovska, IMS VI, Scupi et la région de Kumanovo, Beograd 1982 nos. 58, 59.

[77] M. Mirković, Military Diplomas from Viminacium and the Settlement of auxiliary veterans: city or countryside? In Kaiser, Heer und Gesellschaft in der Römischen Kaiserzeit, Gedenkenschrift für Eric Birley, ed. G. Alföldy, B. Dobson, W. Eck, Stuttgart, 2000, 365-375.

[78] See S. Link, Konzepte der Privilegierung römischer Veteranen, Heidelberger Althistorische Studien Bd. 9, Stuttgart 1989. Regarding the papyrus testifying the fiscal privileges of the auxiliary veteran see M. Mirković, Roman military diplomas, epistulae and papyrological evidence, Proceedings of the 20th Intern. Cong. Of Papyrologists, Copenhagen 23-29 August 1992, 425-455.

[79] AE 1950, no. 44. Up. G. Alföldy, Bevölkerung, 135 and J.J. Wilkes, Dalmatia, 112 i d.

[80] G. Alföldy, Die Auxiliartruppen der Provinz Dalmatien, Mavors Roman Army Researches, III, 1987, 269 i 280-285.

Two waves of colonization in the municipium could be assumed; one from the coastal zone in Dalmatia, from the Rider and Vrlike region, on the deserted or scarcely inhabited land in the Lim and Ćehotina valley, if not on behalf of the emperor, then under official supervision, and the second without being planned movement, but carried out individually on the *ager publicus* on the city territory by the former soldiers of the auxiliary units. Both are separated by a short interval of time. One more reason to assume that former soldiers lived on the city territory is the discovery of money struck at Viminacium in the third century for the payment of soldiers.[81]

City territory

Ilijino Brdo

The city territory of Municipium spreading out in the Ćehotina valley reached on the west probably the river Lim. Roman monuments, graves and inscriptions have been found in Radosavac, Podpec, Ljutić, Otilovići and Gradac (Meitef). It could be assumed that all these spots belonged to the city territory of Municipium as well as the places between Pljevlja and another another big Roman settlement near Prijepolje, on the bank of the river Lim, at Seljani, Seljašnica, Džurovo, Radoinja and Derikonjici.

The most important, probably native settlement, on the city territory was situated on the Ilijino Brdo (Sveti Ilija hill), in the southern edge of the Ćehotina valley, about 5 km distant from Municipium in Komini.

Hoernes was the first to publish the Roman inscriptions from Sveti Ilija hill, together with those found in Pljevlja in 1867.[82] Evans described the monuments from Sveti Ilija hill and other remains which he saw in 1877. His description, Antiquarian researches, p. 32, bears ground to suppose that the native settlement was situated on the hill: "That the spot had been used for purposes of interment from pre-historic times, appears from the remains of its neighborhood of *gomilas* or stone barrows, of the kind common throughout these regions, and dating, as their contents show, from the Illyrian Iron Age [---]. The sepulture thus early begun was continued at this spot after the Roman conquest. The southern end of the hill of St. Ilija is literally undermined with graves and the recurrence of native names on the sepulchral slabs of Roman date that have been discovered shows that those who under the Roman Empire continued to bury their dead here were essentially of the same indigenous race as the barrow/builders who had gone before them. The remains were for the most part originally encased in pinewood coffins traces of which are still to be seen; and these again were enclosed in rude stone cists, the direct descendants of the more massive cists to be found inside the 'gomile'. On some cases the skeletons actually occur in a contracted posture, a primitive usage characteristic of the earliest Stone-Age interments". The archaeological investigations which could prove this observations have not been done until now.

Evans assumed that an Illyrian center existed on Sveti Ilija height before the Romans came. In order to underline the difference between the Roman town near Pljevlja and native settlement on Sveti Ilija hill, he describes the monuments at Plejvlje on one hand as being of characteristic Roman execution (p. 30), with letters and ornamentation which comes up to the usual municipal standards. The inscriptions refer to the civic officers, priests and legionaries, citizens, for the most part with the Roman names / *Aelius* and *Aurelius*. Evans believes that Municipium was founded in Hadrian's time, and enlarged by fresh settlement of veterans in the age of the Antonines. The monuments on the hill Sveti Ilija on the other hand are of different character. They are of a ruder and more barbaric style, and the strikingly large proportion of the names are native Illyrian. As Evans observes the walls and pavement of the little church are largely composed of ancient monuments, amongst which Illyro-Roman sepulchral slabs predominate (p. 33). He remarks that among these the style of workmanship and decoration is rude "almost to grotesqueness" as of the monument fig. 13; the upper part of the stone containing the busts is bedded into the pavement of the atrium; the lower part with the inscription was bedded into the pavement of the church itself (CIL III 6347). Opposite the west door of the church stand a huge sepulchral block of cubical form with a gabled top (p. 35, 14). with the Cyrilian inscription that means that it was adopted for sepulchral purposes later. Its front face contains the busts of a man and his wife of "barbarian execution", whiles on the sides are carved two genii, one with a raised, the other with a lowered torch. and wearing Phrygian caps.. In the fundaments of the pope's house burnt by the Turks, below the church, on the southern slope of the hill, Evans saw many ancient monuments, among other the dedication to the Caesar Diadumenian which was used as one of stone posts of the stable-door. (p. 36, fig. 15).

There is no doubt that Ilijino Brdo was on the city territory of Municipium in Komini. *Ordo decurionum* from Municipium was entitled to give permission to erect the monument dedicated to the emperor, as the clause *loco dato decreto decurionum* proves:

18. Slab of limestone height 108 width 60 thick 33 cm. found on Ilijino brdo, reused as one of the stone posts of the stable door near the pope house on the slope of the hill.

Hoernes, AEM 4, 1880, 191; Evans, Antiquarian Researches, 1885, 36, with drawing fig. 15; Patsch, GMBH 6, 1894, 479, with drawing 19 and WMBH 6, 1896, no. 27, with drawing 63; CIL III 8307 + p. 2255.

[[M. Opellio | Antonino | Diadumeni|ano nobilis|simo caes|ari principi | i[uv]en[tut]is Caes(aris) [M.] | Ope[l]l[ii Se]veri Ma|crini p(ii) f(elicis) A[ug(usti) fil(io) | p(ecunia) p(ublica) d(ecreto) d(ecurionum).

---
[81] The information of M. Ružić. The numismatic material is now in the Archaeological Collection of the Filozofski fakultet in Belgrade.
[82] Hoernes, AEM 4, 1880, 191.

Line 7: *Imp. Caes.* Evans.

From the year 217/218

The inscritions from Ilijino Brdo reffer to civic officers, legiony soldier and citizens. *Duovir* and *quinquennalis* was M. Aemilius Titiannus (no. **4**) from the *Aemilii* family which gave another *duovir* in the Municipium, Aemilius Antonius whose monument was found at Pljevlja (no. **3**). the latter was mentioned on the monument of Aemilius Calvinus who died in Salona.

Altar to two Augusti was dedicated by *populus*.

19. Altar partly cracked in the middle; found on Ilijino Brdo.

Blau, Acta acad. Berol. 1866, 846; CIL III 6340=8303; Hoernes, AEM IV, 1880, 187; Evans, Antiquarian Researches 37, with drawing, fig. 16.

I(ovi) O(ptimo) M(aximo) | Advento et | pro salute et v(i)c|(to)ñas (!) imp(eratorum duorum) | Âug(ustorum duorum) populus | p(osuit)

Line 3: SALVE Evans; line 4: /asimpp// Blau, ÎKAS INPP //// Evans, ÎRASIM Hoern; line 5: //NC//P Blau, s/a///o/// Hoernes, completed in *S[t]a[necl]o[rum]*, omitted by Blau. Inspecting the stone Evans recognized P on the basis. However his assumption that the altar was dedicated to *procurator* seems not to be acceptable.

Precise dating of the monument is not possible; two Augusti could be Marcus Aurelius and Lucius Verus, but also Septimius Severus and Caracalla as well as many other emperors.

The expected clause on the end *loco dato decreto decurionum* is omitted. Instead appears *populus*. The meaning of the word is manifold. It could design the *populus* of the city in general, that means the *municipes*, or the natives organized in the *civitas* with their center on Ilijino Brdo. *Populi* in Pliny, n.h. are peoples in Latium outside Rome; *populus* in Spain could mean the assembly of all free men without any difference whether the community was of Roman or Latin right;[83] *senatus* and *populus* are the main institutions also in the peregrine communities in the provinces in the time of Republic and the Principate. About the aborigine people in this region and its organization is not known much. May be the *populus* in the quoted inscription from Ilijino Brdo has the meaning of *civitas*. Still it seems more probably to assume that *populus* was used to designate the same as *municipes*. Natives from Ilijino Brdo, even if they were organized as *civitas*, have had their organization in cult and religion, but they could not be an independent community. Even if they were *civitas*, they were attributed to the Municipium.[84] That means that they made part of the city population. All together they decided to erect the monument to the regnant emperors.

There are good reasons to believe that the agglomeration on the Ilijino brdo stayed predominantly native even in the Roman times, as Evens concluded. This assumption is based on the frequency of Illyrian names in the inscriptions found there. *Germanus, Panto, Testo, Trito, Titto,* are included in the middle Dalmatian group by R. Katičić. *Germanus* appears in the inscriptions in Rider, Panto is common Illyrian spread in the coastal zone and in many places n the interior of the Province, among others in many places around Pljevlja, in Komini and Podpeć[85] and in the inscriptions from Kolovrat near Prijepolje; the middle Dalmatian name *Testo* appears in Sveti Ilija hill. Katičić, MDN 277 who knows two samples from Pljevlja, brings the name in connection with the name of the Dalmatian first mentioned by App. Illyr. 26, 27; *Titto/Tito*, appears in Pljevlja and Prijepolje and in the coastal zone in Vrlike and in the region of Siculi;[86] Tritano appears on the monuments in Komini, but also in Rider, *Trito* as attested in Kolovrat.[87] All these names are wide spread in Dalmatia, but especially concentrated in Rider, Vrlike, Pljevlja and Prijepolje. On IlijinoBrdo they appear in the following monuments:

20. Five fragments of the limestone slab joining one another. On the top two human busts are represented in the profiled frame. It was found on the left of the church on Sveti Ilija hill

Patsch, WMBH IV, 1896, p. 288, no. 33 with drawing fig. 69.

D(is) M(anibus) | Germano | q(ui) v(ixit) an(nos) XV | Ni[ ] | filio p(ater) p(osuit)

21. Three fragments of the limestone slab, a) the part of the upper right corner height 85, width 62 thick 32 cm, decorated with three damaged, difficult recognizable, bust in the arch on the top. b) parts of the left upper corner height 62 width 37 thick 32 m c) not measured fragment with the hole on the lower part. The inscription was difficult to read in the time when seen by Patsch. It was found in front of the church on Ilijino Brdo.

Patsch, GZM 6, 1894, 485 and idem, WMHB 4, 1896. 289, no. 36 with drawing fig.. 72; CIL III 12716

D(is) M(anibus) s(acrum) [?Pan]toni [....]vunxi [f(iliae)....] Sup(er?) coniugi b(ene) m(erenti) et] sibi v[ivus pos(uit). Patsch.

It has been restored the name, *Di]toni, Tes]toni, Tit]oni* and similar in line 2.

22. Funerary slab of limestone, height 162 width 85 thick 32 cm. In the upper part in the arch are represented two

---

[83] H. Galsterer, Untersuchungen zum römischen Stäftewesen auf der iberischen Halbinsel, 1971. Cf. A. Stylow, *Decemviri*, ein Beitrag zur Verwaltung peregriner Gemeinden in der Hispania Ulterior, Ciudad y Comunidad en Hispania – siglos 3 y 3d.C. / Madrid 1993, 37.

[84] A.N. Sherwin White, The Roman Citizenship² 1873, 8, 48 i passim.

[85] See the ch. about the native names, p. 44 ff.
[86] Katičić, MDN 282.
[87] Katičić, MDN 278.

human figures, left feminine, right masculine. Found immured in the wall of the Sveti Ilija church.

Blau, Acta Acad, Ber. 1866, 848 (CIL III 8364); Hoernes, AEM 4, 1880. 188, no. 13 (CIL III 8326); Patsch, GZM 6, 1894, no. 34 and idem, WMBH 4, 1896. p. 288, no. 34; CIL III 8326.

D(is) M(anibus) S(acrum) | Sex. Statius | Restitutus | sibi et Aureliae | Testoni coniugi | posuit.

Line 2: SIX Blau line 3: RESTIVIVS Blau Line 4: /IBI E AURELIAE Blau Line 5: CONIV Blau, Hoernes.

23. Fragment of the funerary slab immured in the church of Sveti Ilija. Lost.

Hoernes, AEM 4, 1880, p. 191; CIL III 8327.

D(is) M(anibus) S(acrum) Val(eriae) Te[stoni?] qu(a)e v(ixit) [ann(nos)...] Ae(lius) Qu[intus ma]tri

24. Funerary slab inmured in the church pavement on Ilijino Brdo. Noted in 1866, later lost; Hoernes didn't see it in 1880.

Blau, Acta Acad. Berol. 1866, 848, 11; CIL III 6350 = 8319.

D(is) M(anibus) s(acrum) | Aureliae Tittoni | quae v(ixit) a(nnis) | XLV Aur(elius) Carus c(oniugi) | b(ene) m(erenti) p(osuit)

25. Three fragments of the same (?) funerary slab of the dark limestone which don't fit together. Found on Ilijino Brdo.

Patsch, GZM 6, 1894, 48 nd idem, WMBH IV, 1896, p. 287, no. 32 with drawing fig. 68; CIL III 13851.

Patsch reconstructed the following text:

Ḍ(is) [M(anibus)] | Aur̞(elio) [---] | et Ti[ttoni? | [q]u[ae vix(it) an(nos) | [coniugi ?] eius Cami[a? | p(arentibus) et [s]ibi viva [p(osuit)].

26. Limestone funerary slab height 38 width 86 cm. The inscribed field in the profiled frame. It was noted as immured in the Sveti Ilija church, on the right of the entrance.

CIL III 8320; Patsch, WMBH 4, 1896, p. 287, no. 31, with drawing.

D(is) M(anibus) s(acrum) | Aur(eliae) Trita|noni q(uae) v(ixit) an(nos) | XXX Aur(elius) Maxsi|mus (!) coniugi [....

27. Funerary monument immured in Sveti Ilija church. Lost.

Blau, Acta Acad. Berol. 1866, 848, 12 (CIL III 6352); Hoernes, AEM 4, 1880, 188, no. 12; CIL III 8321.

D(s) M)anibus) S(acrum) | Aur(eliae) Vendoni | q(uae) v(ixit) a(nnis) XXIII T. Aur(elius) VS[ ].

28. Funerary slab. Found on Ilijino Brdo.

Patsch, AEM 16, 1893, 88; CIL III 12783; Patsch, GZM 6, 1894, 482, no. 35 and WMBH 4, 1896, 288, no. 35 with drawing fig. 71; CIL III 13813.

D(is) M(anibus) s(acrum) | Terenti | q(ui) vix(it) an(nos) LX | et Vend|oni con|iugi aeius (!)| vive (!) Bes|sus par(entibus) p(ro) | p(ietate) et sibi | vius (!) p(osuit).

All names, *Terens, Vendo* and *Bessus* are of native origin.

29. Funerary monument of limestone height 25 width 74 thick 30 cm. Inscribed field in the profiled frame; above is represented a rose. It was seen in Ilijino brdo, immured in the stable on the left of the entrance.

Blau, Mitteilungen acad, Berol. 1866, 849; Hoernes, AEM 4, 1896, 188, 11; Patsch, GZM 6, 1894, 479 and WMBH 4, 1896, p. 286, no. 29; CIL III 8315. Cf. Sergejevski, Spomenik 98, 1941/48, 145.

D(is) M(anibus) s(acrum) | Au̞r(elio) A[p]ro | qui vixit | an(nos) XXXX | Lucida | coiugi pie|ntissimo | p(osuit).

30. Funerary slab, broken in the middle. On the upper part represented four busted in arches one above another, two in each of them. It was found near the Sveti Ilija church.

Blau, Acta acad, Berol. 1866, 849; Hoernes, AEM 4, 1896,189; Evans, Antiquarian Researches, 34; Patsch, GZM 6, 1894, 480 and idem, WMBH 4, 1896, p. 286-7, no. 30; CIL III 8314 (= 6347).

D(is) M(anibus) s(acrum) | Aur(elio) Ap|ro q(ui) v(ixit) an(nos) L | et Aur(elia) Ca[n]|dida [viva?] | coiu[x eius?]

31. Funerary slab.

Blau, Acta Acad. Berol. 1866, 848, 14.

D(is) M(anibus) s(acrum) | Aur( ) Ap| lo? or Ap|ro q(ui) (vixit) ani[s]| et AI[..] |DIE[...] |con(iugi) [...].

32. Fragment of the funerary monument of limestone, brocken in three parts, height 96 width 73 thick 23 cm. Patsch saw it in front of the church on Sveti Ilija hill.

Patsch, GZM 6, 1894, 479 and idem, WMBH 4, 1896, 286, no. 28 with drawing; CIL III 13850. Cf. Vulić, Spomenik 98, 1941-48, p. 145.

Ḍ(is) Ṃ(anibus) | L. Ae[(l(io) ....]ntio filio | piissimo qui vixit | annos XIII Herma et [5] | Martia parentes | ipsi sibi | in memori|am posuerunt.

Line 2 *Ama]ntio* Patsch, adding as other possibilities, *Aude]ntio, Fide]ntio, Leo]ntio, Po]ntio* etc.

The family could be of servile origine.

33. Fragment of the limestone funerary monument. Found on Ilijino Brdo.

Hoernes, AEM 4, 1880, p. 191, no. 2; CIL III 8312; Patsch, GZM 6, 1894, no. 37 and idem, WMBH 4, 1896, 1889, no. 37.

Ael(ius) Bessus et | Ael(ia) Ursa fil(iae) pientissime (!) et | sibi vivi p(osuerunt).

The name *Bessus* could be of Thracian origin.

34. Fragment of the limestone funerary monument, immured in the doorstep in the Sveti Ilija church.

Blau, Acta Acad. Berol. 1866, 849, 19; CIL III 6357; Hoernes, AEM 4, 1880, 189, no. 20.

] et Fusca M D | [ ] et sibi viva | [ ] p(osuit)

line 1: PIVS.ANN, 2 VIVAI Blau, et Fuscam D CIL.

The name *Fuscus/a* could be of native origin. See *Ana Fuscae*, no. 43; a soldier of the legion *XIII Gemina* was burried Ilijino brdo:

35. Funerary monument height 195 width 41 cm. The soldier is represented with a sward and shield. Inscribed field in the profilled frame. Found on the Ilijino brdo.

Kubitschek, VHAD n.s. XV, 1928, p. 38 f. no. 4 with drawing Abb. 4 (A. et J. Šašel, ILJug. 1730).

D(is) M(anibus) | Âe(lio) Felicia|no mi(liti) le(gionis) | XIII Ge(minae) q(ui) v(ixit) a(nnis) | XXV filio| dul(cissimo) Maxi|mus êt Fi|aêtia p(arentes).

Letters height 3.5 – 5 cm.

Line 7/8: Fi|...a Kubitschek; Fiaetia, assuming as possible names *Firma* or *Finita*.

The name *Fiaetia* is unknown.

Evans and Patsch noted many bricks with stamps M R and A S found on Ilijino Brdo hill. The same bricks are discovered in Komini.

Other places on city territory

Find spots of the monuments in the region close are not numerous.

An altar dedicated have been discovered in the cottage **Radosavac**.

36. Small altar of limestone was immured in the house of Čifči Jestrović.

CIL III 8305; N. Vulić, Spomenik 98, 1941/1948, 145, no. 313 photo made by Sergejevski.

S.A.S

It could be completed in *S(ilvano) A(ugusto) s(acrum)*

37. Limestone funerary slab was found in the village **Podpeć**, on the south of Pljevlja in the village cemetery. In the upper part two portraist are represented.

Evans, Antiquarian researches 1885, 42, with drawing, fig 19; CIL III 8318; N. Vulić, Spomenik 98, 1941-1948, no. 312 with photo made by D. Sergejevskog (A. et J. Šašel, ILJug. 1709).

D(is) M(anibus) S(acrum) | Aur[elia] | Panto [s(ibi) v(iva)] | et Aur[el(iae)--- | toni q(uae) v(ixit) a(nnis) --] b(ene) [m(erenti) p(osuit)].

Line 3-4 *Tes]toni* Evans.

38. In the village **Ljutić** near Mataruge in the region of Pljevlja on the land possession of Milun Ćirović was discovered 1983 damaged limestone funerary monument height 105 width 60 thick 25 cm. Inscribed field decorated with vine and leaves. In the upper part a human bust with drinking cup on his breast and the ivy leave in his hand. Broken in two; major part of the inscription is wipe out.

M. Lazić and M. Cerović, Rimski grob iz Ljutića, Glasnik srpskog arheološkog društva 8, 1992, 105-109, with photo.

D(is) M)anbus) | [.......]us | [ ] | Ianuarius | f(liae or -o?) p(osuit).

39. In the village **Gradac**, on the place called Meitef was recently discovered a funerary slab of limestone. In the upper part three busts under the arch. The surface badly damaged, the inscription wiped out. Dimensions are 160 x 87 x 30 cm.

J. Cvijetić, Rimski nadgrobni spomenik iz Gradca kod Plevalja, Glasnik srpskog arheološkog društva, 25, 2009, 141-147.

[.........]VS NOVI |[...] Maximu[s]| [filio?] pient(issimo)| [ ]patri |...MI vixit an XXX |...vivi et III | alumno? et Rufin(o) vi |vis f(ecit.|

Cvijetić reads:

[---] | [+-6] NOV [.] |[+- 5] Maximus | [+- 11] pien[to]|^5[is]simi nept[es? +-7]| [+-2]MOV vivi et [+-5] Samiano et Rufinus v(ivi) i(psi) s(ibi) f(ecerunt].]

Samiano should be the Illyrian femininum –o.

40. During the archeological investigation 2010 in Otilovići, about 6 km on the East of Pljevlja, has been discovered a Roman funerary monument reused as the doorstep of the early Christian church which was built here probably in the later Roman times, not fare from the prehistoric tomb (tumulus).

Limestone funerary monument height 173 with 60 thick 32 cm. Letters height 2-6 cm. In the upper part two busts, female with the scarf on her head and an and male.

J. Cvijetić, Starinar (to be printed).

D(is) M(anibus) S(acrum) | Pleto|r(i) Maxi|mina vi|va sibi f(ecit) e|t Victor|ino et Stat|ie (!) Fuscinie f|lie (!) car(issimae) pi|ent(issimae) b.m. | marito,

Pletor is the Illyrian name (Mayer, Ill. Sprache 274). It appears also in Alburnus Maior in Dacia where a part of Pirustae, as it was supposed, have been transported to work in the mines. The wife and children bear the Roman names. Only the daughter has the gentile *Statia*, frequent in the Municipium and surroundings. Her name *Fuscina* similar to Fusca appears also in the inscriptions in this region (*Ana Fusca*, no. **43**) and on the hill Ilijino Brdo (no. **35**) and in the rest of the province Dalmatia as well as in Italy and the western provinces of the Empire.[88]

Names in the inscriptions from the region around Pljevlja show clearly that on the city territory lived the same people as in the city. The Illyrians must be an important component in it, as the names *Panto* (no. **37**) and *Pletor* (no. **40**) prove

41. In Otilovići has been found a milestone, height 68, diameter 33 and 27 cm in upper part. down 37 cm. Discovered in the cemetery in Otilovići, reused as the Christian funeral monument Now in the Museum in Prijepolje.

Sergejevski, Spomenik XCVIII, 1940, no. 22, with photo.

Imp(eratori) Gai<u>o Iulio | Vero Macximino (!) | p(io) f(elici) et G. Iulio Vero | Macximo (!) <i>nob(illissimo) Caes(ari) Aug(usto) C(aesari) n(ostri) P? Augg(us|tis) n(ostris).

On this spot was probably situated a station on the road connecting the Roman Municipium in Komini and the settlement in Kolovrat near Prijepolje.

d) CITY POPULATION: ROMAN CITIZENS, PEREGRINI AND FOREIGNERS

There was no strict division between the Romans and natives in the municipium. Illyrian names appear in the Roman families and both Romans citizens and those of Illyrian origin were buried side by side in necropolis II at Komini. The tombs and graves in the central part of necropolis II were occupied for the most part by the Romanized people and their families.

---
[88] Lörincz, Onomasticon, s.v.

Natives also lived on the city territory in the surroundings of the city as *peregrini*, i.e. as people who did not enjoy Roman civil rights. Roman citizens also owned land in the city surroundings. A native family appears on the monument found in Otilovići (no. **40**); Romans or Romanized were discovered on the monument from Ljutići (no. **38**). The basic difference between Roman citizens and peregrines were unequal fiscal obligations. Roman citizens enjoyed the privilege of paying lower state and city taxes. Reduced taxes were also paid by veterans who settled in the provinces.

Roman citizens as well as the *peregrini*, all those born in the city and permanently settled in the city or on the city territory, were registered in the city tax registers which were controlled every fifth year. The third category of city dwellers were *incolae*, those born and registered in other cities but temporarily settled down in the municipium. They were further obliged to pay basic taxes in their native town, but they could have some obligations (liturgies, municipal taxes) and also enjoy certain privileges in the place where they lived temporarily, as the papyrological evidence from Egypt proves. In the time of *lustrum* every five years, they were obliged to return to their birth place in order to declare their possession and their person.

The data on inscriptions from the municipium proves the same structure of the city population as in other provincial cities. The town and its surroundings were inhabited by *cives Romani*, who were born as *cives* or were granted Roman citizenship from the emperors in the second and third centuries, by *peregrini* as natives without Roman citizenship, and *incolae* who lived there temporarily attracted by different reasons. All together are attested in the inscription found immured in the Sveta Trojica church near Pljevlje:

42. Limestone base or altar: height 101, width 47.5 cm. Discovered in the basement of the column in the interior of the church during the restoration works in 2000.

S. Loma, Zbornik muzeja Pljevlja 3, 2002 and the same, Živa antika 52, 2002, 146-147 (AE 2002, 1115); P. Le Roux, ZPE 154, 2005, 261-266 (AE 2005, 1183).

Sexto Aur(elio) Lupiano | Lupi filio princip(i) | decuriones collegae et populares | et peregrini incolae civi optimo ob merita | pos(uerunt) | epulo dedicata (ara? statua?) *l(oco) d(ato) d(ecreto) d(ecurionum)*

Reading involves no great difficulty. It is to be noted that *dedicata* as femininum in line 6 cannot be connected with neutrum *epulo* that follows. It must concern the omitted word *ara* or *statua* in the formulation like in the inscription from Salona, CIL III 1933: *hanc aram Iuppiter Optime Maxime do dico dedico...* etc.

It is not possible to discover where the monument was found before it was used as building material in the nineteenth century. It could be assumed that it was erected on city territory. The municipium in Komini is the nearest city to Sveta Trojica. *Lco dato decreto decurionum* indicates that the monument devoted to Sextus Aurelius Lupianus was erected on the city territory belonging to the municipium in Komini.

The inscription deserves more extensive comment on one hand because its value was overestimated when first published and because it was falsely interpreted as concerning the process of the attribution of the native community to the Roman city.[89] On the other hand, it is not necessary to call for Greek parallels in explaining the terms and words in it[90] since all of the terms used in the text are known elsewhere in the Roman world.

The text mentions different groups of inhabitants but its contribution to the investigation even of the relationship between different social groups in the city territory is rather modest. *Sextus Aurelius Lupianus Lupi filius*, to whom the statue or altar was dedicated, was qualified in the inscription as *civis optimus*. He was probably of native origin. He or his predecessors were granted Roman citizenship under the emperor Marcus, as his name Aurelius indicates. His father's name, Lupus, and his cognomen Lupianus, like Lupercus and similar, derives from *lupus* (wolf, she-wolf) the animal which plays a prominent role in the foundation myth of Rome. *Aelius Lupercus* was the son of *preafectus civitatis* Aelius Carvanio in inscription no. **1b**. Sextus Aurelius Lupianus was *princeps*. The title was common in the inscriptions in the Roman provinces and in Dalmatia. *Principes* could fulfill their function in a peregrine community, but also in castellum or in the Roman city. In the first case the title was followed by the name of the *civitas*, as for instance Ti. Claudius who was *princeps Delmatarum* (CIL III 2776), Gaius Epicadi f. was *princeps civitatis Docleatium*, but his relative *Agirius Epicadi f.* was *princeps castelli*;[91] Bato was *princeps Daesitiatium* in the time of the Dalmatiian revolt in AD 6-9,[92] and there are many others in the Balkan provinces.[93] The crucial word, which defines his function, is missing in this case. This is why it seems less likely that Sextus Aurelius Lupianus was *princeps* of the peregrine *civitas*. There is one more reason for doubt: native *civitates* and tribes in the region of Pljevlja and Prijepolje were preceded by *praefectus civitatis* as inscription no. **1b** testifies. Another function which appears in this region was *curator*. In an inscription from Pljevlja a Roman citizen of the equestrian order appears as *curator* of four different ethnic groups *Arbenses, Metlenses, Splonistae* and *Malvesatii* (no. **2**).[94]

Other possibility is to understand under *princeps* an office in the city. The title *princeps municipii* occurs in the inscriptions from the cities in Dalmatia, for instance in one from Rider CIL III 2774, where he was qualified as *quinquennalis*: *D(is) M(anibus) Q. Rutilio Q.f. Titiano II vir(o) q(uin)q(uennali) et Q. Rutilio Q.f. Proculo II vir(o) q(uin)q(uennali) filio eius principi municipi Riditarum*.[95] The title *quinquennalis* links him with *lustrum* and taxes. *Princeps coloniae* is attested in Salona, CIL III 9540. *Princeps* appears in an inscription from Oescus in Moesia Inferior as a leader in the city council, CIL III 14416: *T. Aurelio T. Fil. Papir. Flaviano primi pilari et principi ordinis col(oniae) Osesc(ensi) et buleuta civitatius Tyranorum, Dionysiop(oli). Marcianopoli, Tungrorum et Aquincensium* etc. It could be assumed that Sextus Aurelius Lupianus was a *princeps* in a city. He was named a *collega* by city decurions, as formulated *expressis verbis* in the inscription. The monument was dedicated by *decuriones* to their *collegae*. The word *collegae*, either dativus singularis or nominativus pluralis, expresses the same: he was one of the city decurions to whom they dedicated monuments and arranged the *epulum*. He could have been entrusted with a special mission, as princeps in the inscription from Dacia, CIL III 1322: *Aur. Afer Delmata princ(eps) adsignato(!) ex (municipio) Splono*. His mission on the territory of the municipium could be linked with *lustrum* and taxes in the community of *peregrini* and *incolae*. The jurisdiction of the city magistrates on the territory inhabited by peregrini is well known. Numerous inscriptions found in Bölcske, near Aquincum, on the territory of Eravisci, document among others the city *duoviri* as being responsible for erecting altars to Jupiter in the name of the *civitas Eraviscoum*.[96]

Decuriones were entrusted with the erection of the monument and the organization of the solemn feast on behalf of the community and in the name of their *ordo* and the people, of *populares* and *peregrini incolae*. It was the common duty of the community designed as *decuriones* and *populus, coloni, incolae, cives, municipes*, and is a well documented practice in the Roman world: *populo*, CIL II 5514; CIL VII 1574, *colonis et liberis eorum et incolis*, CIL IX 2252, *municipibus et incolis utriusque sexus*, CIL XI 5693, *civibus*, CIL VIII 767, *civibus et incolis*, CIL II 2100, *cenam decurionibus et filiis eorum et plebi*, CIL IX 2962, *epulum populo et decurionibus*, and others.[97]

The words *populares* and *peregrini incolae* in the inscription from Sveta Trojica relate to the city population which was of the same structure as other cities in the provinces and consisted of Roman citizens, native

---

[89] S. Loma, Princeps i peregrini incolae u municipijumu S(plonistarum?) Živa antika 52. 2002. 143-179) discussed the inscription as proving the atributio of the local tribe to the Roman city.
[90] P. Le Roux, Peregrini incolae, ZPE 154, 2005, 261-266, claims that the term *peregrini incolae* is the same as the Greek ξενοι οι παροικοι, while *colegae decuriones* corresponds to the Greek synbouleutai (p. 265).
[91] Vulić, Spomenik 71, 1931, 241-242.
[92] Vulić, Spomenik 98, 1941-1948, 10.
[93] *Princeps civ[itatis] Dinda[riorum]* G. Alföldy, Bevölkerung, 50, 53, 56, 97, 159; *principes* (CIL III 14324), and also *praepositi* and *principes* (CIL III 14326) are attested by the Japodes. *Princeps* also appears in the powerful Pannonian tribes; Azali (AE 1937, 138), Scordisci, Eravisi, Boi and Taurisi. See Mócsy, RE S.IX, 609 ff.
[94] About praefectus and *princeps* see G. Alfoldy, Bevölkerung, 176.
[95] D. Rendić-Miočević, Princeps municipii Riditarum, Iliri i antički svijet, Split, 1989. 853-869.
[96] J. Beszédes, Zs. Mrav, Tóth E., Die Steindenkmäler von Bölcske – Inschriften und Sculpturen, Römische Inschriften und Funde, Budapest 2003, 103 ff. Inscriptions no. 2, 4, 6, 7 and others.
[97] See examples in Rugg. Diz. Epigr. S.v. *epulum*, 2143.

peregrini and peregrini temporarily settled on the city territory. Both terms are well known in literary and epigraphic texts but are not usually linked together. *Populares*, presumably the same as *populus*, could mean the people in general or all the inhabitants of a specific city, or part of it. *Populi* were all peoples subject to Rome in Italy and in the provinces.[98] *Populus* appears in inscription no. **19** found on the hill Ilijino Brdo. If equal in meaning to *populus*, *populares* in the inscription from Sveta Trijica could mean all the inhabitants registered in the city, both Roman citizen and natives. The term *populares* is used in a similar way by Sallust in *Jugurta* 7.1 and III 2: *non populares modo sed Ausetanos quoque, vicinam gentem concitatae*. *Populares* are Roman citizens and natives in the province, in contrast to the tribe of Ausetani living on the other side of the Roman frontier. The difference between *populares* as those included in the defined community and the others who are outside it is clear defined in Cicero, Leg. I 61: *populares* are the citizen of one place, whereas the others are citizens of the world, *non circumdatur moenibus popularem alicuius definiti loci, sed civem totius mundi*. Interpreted in this sense the *populares* in the inscription from Sveta Trojica are the inhabitants of the city as opposed to the peregrine, new comers or strangers, *peregrini incolae*. *Populares* as those living in the town has the same meaning as *populus* or *municipes*. *Decuriones et populares* in the inscription corresponded to *senatus populusque* in Rome, to *ordo et populus, decuriones et populus, ordo et cives, ordo* or *decuriones et plebs, decuriones municipesque* in the numerous inscriptions in the provinces.[99] The quoted text from Sallust's Jugurta allows us to assume that the term *populares* could mean not only *cives Romani*, but all those who are integrated in one community, including the *peregrini*. In the city like that of the the municipium in Komini, *populares* could have the same meaning as *populus*, i.e. all those registered in the tax registers, *cives Romani* and *peregrini*.

Peregrini incolae were not included in the category of the city populations permanently settled on the city territory. *Peregrini* were not *cives Romani*, which means they were natives without Roman civil rights; the term *incolae* could be applied to both the people without Roman rights as well as to *cives*. It has no political connotation, in Italy or in the provinces. *Incola* does not concern the *status civitatis*. *Incola* is everyone who lives outside his place of *origo*, i.e. outside the city where he was registered. *Incola* could be *peregrinus* as well as *civis* as illustrated by inscription ILS 6088: *Incolae qui cives Romani Latinive cives erunt Malacae*.

No one could be proclaimed *incola*,[100] but anybody could be *incola*, as long as he lived outside his native city. He had his *origo* in one city, and his *domicilium* in another. Juristic texts clearly define the position of an *incola*, as for instance Dig. 30,16 (from the year 239): *incola est qui aliqua regione domicilium suum contulit, quam Graeci παροίκον appellant*, and further: *nec tantum hi, qui in oppido morantur, incolae sunt, sed etiam qui alicuius oppidi finibus ita agrum habent, ut in eo se quasi in aliquam sedem recipiunt* ('An *incola* is one who only dwells in some region, which the Greeks call *paroikos*. *Incolae* are not only those dwelling in one settlement, but also those who own land inside the boundaries of the settlement where they were allowed to live'). The position of an *incola*, either Roman citizen or peregrine, is defined from the aspect of his duty and tax payments. *Municipes* are so called because of performing their duty together, but some of them can say that they are *incolae* or have there domicile in many places: Dig. L 1: *Ulpianus libro secundo. Et proprie quidem municipes appelantur muneris participes, recepti in civitatem ut munera nobiscum facerent* and *5. quosdam autem dicere refert pluribus locis eum incolam esse aut domicilium habere*. Their fiscal duties are regulated by many laws, as for instance C.Iust. X 38: *De municipibus et originariis. Imp Antoninus A. Silvano. Cum Byblum origine, incolam autem apud Berytios esse proponis, merito apud utraque civitates muneribus fundi compelleris;* C. Iust. X, 40, *De incolis*, Imp. Antoninus A. Paulino, 1. *Non tibi obest si, cum incola esses, aliquod munus suscepistis modo si ante quam ad alios honores vocareris domicilium transtulisti;* 3. Imp. Diocletians A. *Est verum eos qui in territorium alicuius civitatis commorantur velut incolas ad subeunda munera vel capiendis honores non adstringi.* 5. Imp. Diocletianus A. *Si in patria uxoris tuae vel in qualibet alia domicilium defixisti, incolatus iure ultro te civitatis muneribus obligasti.*

The sole duty of an *incola* was to carry out his business, as Cicero said, Cic. De off. I 123: *atque incolae officium est nihil praeter suum negotium agere*. The inscriptions differentiate between *municipes, coloni* and *cives* as city dwellers on one hand and temporarily settled *incolae* on the other, as CIL IX 2252 or *colonis et liberis eorum et incolis, municipibus et incolis utriusque sexus*, CIL XI 5693, *civibus et incolis*, CIL II 2100. According to Roman law everyone had to pay taxes in the place of his registration. It could be assumed that *peregrini incolae* in the inscription from Sveta Trojica originated from some other city or country, as opposed to the other *peregrini* who had their *origo* in the municipium. *Incolae* are opposite to *cives* who were registered in the city, as formulated in Lex Iulia Genitiva (Bruns, Fontes7 150,II = Dessau, ILS 6818), or to *municipes* CIL V 903, VIII 1641) and *coloni* (CIL III 1933). The structure of the city inhabitants is similar to that in the inscription from Sveta Trojica, with *decuriones, coloni* and *incolae* appearing in an inscription from Salona, CIL III 1933, *ut sis volens propitus mihi collegisque meis decurionibus colonis incolis coloniae Martiae Iuliae Salonae...*[101]

---

[98] A.N. Sherwin White, The Roman Citizenship ², 1973, 8: citizens were initially organised into small villages and the small population was grouped into religious communities. See page 1. 31, 48 i passim. Plinius for instance enumerates fifty three *populi* in Italy.

[99] Up. Ruggiero, Diz. ep. s.v. Decuriones, 1536.

[100] The formulation of S. Loma in her article Princeps i peregrini incolae u municipijumu S(plonistarum?), Živa antika 52, 171 that *incolae* were "politically inferior populations" is unclear. Neither does her assertions that the emperor could grant the status of *incolae* or that "incolae were integrated into the Roman political community", has any sense (p. 161).

[101] For other similar structures see Berger, RE IX A, 1914, 1249-1256. The inscription from north Africa is significant, CIL VIII 23880: *cives*

If applied to the local situation in the municipium in Komini, the inscription from Sveta Trojica could mean that the city and its territory were inhabited by *cives* and *peregrini*, who together could be named *populares* (*municipes*, as they were named in other inscriptions) and *peregrini incolae*. The original *peregrini* were natives in the country and must have been registered in the city together with *cives*. They together made the *populus*. They were not numerous as the archeological investigations prove and probably lived in the rural areas. There is reason to assume the existence of another group of *peregrine* in the municipium who were transported by the Romans in great numbers from the coastal region and settled in the city later. They could be named *peregrini incolae*.

Native names and Roman families in the inscriptions from Municipium and its territory

Large number of Illyrian names appears in the families living in the Roman city at Komini as well as in these whose funeral monuments are discovered in the surroundings. Illyrians appear in the inscriptions as the nearest relatives, wife and mother even in the prominent families as were *Paconii* or *Statii*. However, families in which all members of the family bears Illyrian names are only a few.

F. Krahe in 20s and A. Mayer and D. Detschew in 50s of XX century collected all what is preserved of the Illyrian and Thracian names in the Balkans and elsewhere and represent still the basis of all further study. Celtic names are collected in a Lexicon by A. Holder.[102] Great merit in studying the nomenclature formulas in the inscriptions from Dalmatia belongs to D. Rendić-Miočević.[103] In studies from the 60s of the XX century Illyrian names are divided as typical for special region in the vast territory inhabited by Illyrians, in the South, in the middle and in the North Illyrian names.[104] Important contribution in investigation of all names in the Roman province Dalmatia brings the book of G. Alföldy and his study from the 60s of the twenty century *Die Namengebung der Urbevölkerung in der römischen Provinz Dalmatia*, Beiträge zur Namenforschung 15, 1964.[105] Accepting the division of Illyrian names in three large groups he went a step further in connecting them with specific tribe. Names from the Lim valley and the region of Pljevlja and Prijepolje are separated as one in the middle Dalmatian group which deserves special attention. The majority of them he connected with the names in the region inhabited by the Delmatae. He was the first to recognize certain names in this region as Celtic.

As names could reveal not only the origin and nationality of the person, but also the family relation of the persons mentioned in the inscription, native names in the list that follows are grouped primarily as they appear in different inscriptions and in different families. In order to discover the social connection between the Romans and natives or the family relations, names are not quoted always in the alphabetic order, but as they appear in connection with others in the one or more inscriptions.

Fusca Ana and Iarito Arvi appear together on the sepulchral monument found in Pljevlja.

43. Fragmented gravestone slab, height 51 width 64 cm. It was reused in a stairs in the old Turkish hospital at Pljevlja:

Sergejevski, Spomenik 93, 1940, 23 with photo; Vulić, Spomenik 98, 1941-48, 141, 308, with photo made by D. Sergejevski (A. et J. Šašel, ILJug. 1719);

> *D(is) M(anibus) S(acrm) | Iarito Ar( ) |vi(vus) s(ibi) p(osuit) et | Fuscae Ane | con(iugi) s(uae) d(ulcissimae) q(uae) | v(ixit) an(nis) L.*

Lines 2-3: *Iarito Arvi* Vulić, *Iarito Ar( ) vi(vus) sibi*, Šašel; line 4 *Fuscae Ane(i)*, line 5 *con(iugi) s(uae) d(omine)q(ue)* Vulić, Šašel, *con(servae), con(tubernali)* and similar, as less probably, Šašel.

Ana is considered Illyrian name.[106] A. Mayer, Die Sprache, s.v. quotes among others one from Delphi where Ana is explicitly considered Illyrian, *Ana to genos Illyrion*. Alföldy, PND 150 adds new evidence: the inscription from Vuksan Lekići in Albania, one more from Kastel Šućurac from the coastal zone in Dalmatia and one from Karan in the eastern Dalmatia. In the Roman settlement in Kolovrat near Prijepolje *Ana* appears in two inscriptions: *Ana Severina*, Cermanović-Kuzmanović, Užički zbornik 18, 1989, NO. 4 and again, *Titus Anae Codalianus*, Vulić, Spomenik 98, 21, no. 333. The reading *Annae(i)* is also possible. For *Annaeus* cf. Katićić, SIN 102, with examples from Narona. **Fusca** is considered cognomen by Alföldy, PND 208; the name appears in the Celtic countries and in Italy, and often in Dalmatia, among others in Pljevlja and in the territory of Municipium, in Rosulje, Vulić, Spomenik 77, 1934, no. 21: *Aurelia Fusca* together with *T. Aur. Rufus Belzeius* and in inscription from the hill Ilijino Brdo, no. **30**, as well as in the inscription found in Džurovo near Priboj in the Lim valley, Vulić, Spomenik 98, no. 331: *Aurelio Fus(co) fil., Aurelia Fus[ca] mater*). **Fuscinia** appears in the inscription recently found in Otilovići, no. **40** as *Statia Fuscinia*.

---

et populi universi non solum propriae urbis verum etiam vicinarum Bisicae.

[102] H. Krahe, Lexicon altillyrischer Personennamen, Heidelberg, 1929; A. Mayer, Die Sprache der alten Illyrier, Wien 1957; D. Detschew, Die thrakischen Sprachreste, Wien 1957; A. Holder, Alt-keltischer Sprachschatz, I-III, Leipzig 1894-1916.

[103] D. Rendić-Miočević, Ilirska onomastika na latinskim natpisima Dalmacihe, Split 1948.

[104] R. Katičić, Die illyrischen Personennamen in ihrem südöstlichen Verbeitungsgebiet (SIN), Živa antika 12, 1962, 95-120 i Das mitteldalmatische Namengebiet (MDN), Živa antika 12, 1963, 255-292.

[105] G. Alföldy, Die Personennamen der römischen Provinz Dalmatia, Heidelberg, 1969 (PND); Bevölkerung und Gesellschaft der römischen Provinz Dalmatien, Budapest 1965 (Bevölkerung); Die Namengebung der Urbevölkerung in der römischen Provinz Dalmatia, Beiträge zur Namenforschung 15, 1964.

[106] On the significance of the name *Ana* which could be originaly cognomen or *Lallwort* see D. Rendić-Miočević, Ilirska onomastika 14-15.

The husband's name **Iaritus Ar(vi?)** is also not Latin. It appears in the inscription from the land inhabited by the Celtic-Illyrian tribe of Japodes, in Golubić, Vulić, Spomenik 93, 139. *Ar( )* is not necessarily to be completed in *Arvi*. Possible is also *Ar(genianus)* and *Ar(gurianus)* both known from the inscription found in Pljevlja (see further). Names **Iaro** and **Iaritus** as well as **Arvus** is considered Celtic by Alföldy, BNF 15, 1964 62, who quoted parallels in Holder II 12 f.; Mayer, Ill. Sprache 161 determines *Iaritus* as Illyrian name.

The name **Iaro** appears again in an inscription from Komini.

44. Funerary slab immured in the house of Dušan Preradović in the village Komini. Damaged on all edges. In the upper part is represented the female portrait with scarf on her head. Possible one more bust stand on her side The inscription damaged on the right side

Unpublished. Photo and short notice by A. Cermanović-Kuzmanović, in the Archives of the Archaeological collection of the Faculty of Philosophy in Beograd.

D(is) M(anibus) [S(acrum) ?] | Iaro [.] | RI q(ui) v(ixit) a(nnis) [..] Clem[ ].

The second name is possible to complete in *[A]r(v)i* but also in *[A]r(geniani), [A]r(guriani)*

Line 4: could be completed as *Clem[ens]* or ***Clem[io]***, the latter more probable because the other names in the inscription are native. *Clemio* appears in the native family in Kolovrat, together with *Musta* and *Surillla*, both natives (Mirković, Godišnjak CBI 12, 1975, 99, 6). *Celemio* is attested also in an inscription from Radoinje, Bojanovski, Godišnjak CBI 23, 1989, 147. Alföldy, PND, s.v. qualifies it as typical for the region inhabited by the Delmatae.

The name **Arg( )** appepar only as abbreviation in a monument from Pljevlja:

45. Funeral monument in the form of a large square slab of limestone height 109 width 76 thick 67 cm. Inscribed field on the front side in the profiled frame Letters height 8 to 6 cm. After AE in the last line no trace of further text. Probably left for the wife when she dies. Discovered in 1899 together with three graves when earth slides down from the hill Bijeli Brijeg. The graves were probably part of the Necropolis II at Komini; transported to Pljevlja and exposed in the "Regimentgarten" immured in the exedra of the Alexander's well. Still there.

Patsch, WMBH VIII, 1902, 118, no. 3 with photo fig. 55.

D(is) M(anibus) S(acrum) | Sex. Aure|lius Arg( ) | sibi et Ae( )

Arg( ) could be completed in *Arg(genianus), Arg(urinus)* or *Arg(urianus)*. All three are attested in the inscriptions from Komini and Pljevlja.

Argenianus appears as cognomen of the decurion Aurelius Maximus. He has erected the funerary monument for himself still living and his thirty years old dead daughter Aurelia Maximina. Argenianus was his second cognomen. Two cognomina are frequent in the inscriptions from Pljevlja and Prijepolje.[107]

Arg- could be completed also in Argurianus. This name appears in the feminine form **Arguriana** (Titulla), again as the second cognomen:

46. Funerary monument of limestone height 100 width 55 thick 55. Inscribed field on the front side in the profiled frame. It was immured in the weaver's house in Pljevlja and transported in front of the hotel "Tara" where Vulić saw it.

N. Vulić, Spomenik 71, 1931, no. 284 with photo and idem, Spomenik 98, 1941-1948, 139, no. 305 with photo

D(is) M(anibus) S(acrum) | Aur(eliae) Titullae | Argurianae | que (!) v(ixit) an(nis) LX Aur(elia) ⁵| Titulla Cam|bria amitae | p(ientissimae) p(osuit).

Line 5 *Cameria* Vulić

Amita, a term for the father's sister, in this inscription is one of a few testimonies concerning the kinship system within the extensive family which disappeared later, in the society based on the nuclear family, father, mother, children. The name Arguriana could be connected with the Celtic *Argu-* (Holder I 214 and III 682 f.). The aunt's name *Cambria* is explained as Celtic, as it was *Cambrianus* in the next inscription.[108]

Titulla take the position of Roman cognomen, and as common name of aunt and niece shows clearly that both belonged to the same extensive family. The name is known in Italy and in the provinces.[109] Aurelia is the gentile name accepted when the family was granted the Roman citizenship. To the same root as Cambria belongs the name **Cambrianus** on another monument:

47. Lower part of the Roman altar of limestone height 68 width 79 thick 38 cm. It was immured in the house of Uzejraga Činara at Komini when Vulić saw it.

Vulić, Spomenik 98, 1941-48, 131, no. 289.

[ ] | OL[ ] | Cambrianus | l(ibens) p(osuit).

In Mayer's opinion, Ill. Sprache 177 the name could be Illyrian; for Alföldy, PND 170 the name is of Celtic origin (Holder, I 716 and CIL XIII 4, p. 28). Both, *Cambria* and *Cambrianus* appear only in the inscriptions from Komini.

---
[107] Mirković, Anthropology and epigraphy – the case of Central Balkan region, Acta XII congressus intern. epigraphicae grecae et latinae, 2002, Barcelona 2007, 968 ff.
[108] G. Alföldy, Bevölkerung, 56 i BN 15, 1964, 99.
[109] Lörincz, Onomasticon, s.v.

Close connected with Arguriana is **Argurinus,** the name in the inscription.

48. Fragment of the funeral monument of limestone height 80 width 78 thick 55 cm. Letters height 6-7 cm. In the upper part is represented rose between two palm branches. On both lateral side represented Athis. Inscribed field in the frame Found in the Necropolis II 1975. Preserved in Komini.

Unpublished.

D(is) M(anibus) S(acrum) | Aplis Aur(e)li | Argurinus [---]

The name *Aurelius* in this inscription doesn't take the place of the gentile name, but is used as patronymic, what is unusual in the Roman inscriptions. The buried man was *Aplis* the son of *Aurelius* with the cognomen *Argurinus,* that means the onomastic formula was the personal name, patronymic and cognomen. *Argurinus* could be either the clan name or designed the origin connecting *Aplis* with the extensive family group.[110]

Aplis, Apla appears in the large number of the inscriptions in the region from the Adriatic coast to the central Balkan area, in the middle Dalmatian group of names. The name is frequent in Rider in Dalmatia where are attested 15 samples from 20 known in 1963s while two are from Vrlike.[111] Sample from Pljevlja quoted by him is not certain.[112] Alföldy classified the name *Aplis* as typical for the region inhabited by the Delmatae.[113] *Aplis* appears three times in Pljevlja, once in the soldier's family, no. **16**. He was *T. Aurelius Aplis,* his wife was *Aurelia Vendo* and their son was *T.Aur(elius)Turus.* In the inscription no. **14** feminine form *Apla* is attested as the name of the soldier's wife or daughter. Unusual form had the name in no. **48**: *Aplis Aureli Argurianus.*

Vendo appears further as the wife of *Terens* on the funerary monument which was found on Hill Ilijino Brdo, no. **28**: All names in this family are native: the wife is *Vendo,* her husband is *Terens,* the son is *Bessus.* The last two are not necessary Illyrian.

Terens- *ntis* is attested again in the surroundings of Pljevlja, *Terentoni patri* in the inscription from the village Luzac near Ivangrad (ILJug. 1816). Katičić, MDN 277, determined it as middle Dalmatian name. It have to be strictly distinguish from the Thracian *Teres* in his opinion. *Terens* appears in Vrlike in Dalmatia, *Aurel.*

---

[110] *Argyrianus*, in the inscription on the rock Levertari could be connected with Argenianus. It is not included in the consideration because, firstly, the reading is not sure as shown by drowing by M. Lazića (in the documentation of the Arheological collection at the Filozofski fakultet Beograd, secondly, the rock Levertari is far away from Pljevlje and was probably not insclused in the city territory.
The name Argyrius is attested in Gallia Narbonensis, Argyrus in Dalmatia and Italy (Alföldy, PND 156). *Argyrinoi* are the tribe in Epyros (Mayer, 58).
[111] Katičić, MDN, 263.
[112] CIL III 8314, in which is attested *Aurelius Aper*.
[113] BNF 15, 1964, 81, with a large number of samples.

Terenti. On the contrary Alföldy, PND 307 identifies it with the Thracian *Teres* (Detschew, Thr.Sprachreste, 500 f.). In favor of latter speaks the son's name, **Bessus** which could be of Thracian origin. However *Bessus* is known in the Celtic countries also.

One another **Bessus** appears in the inscription from Ilijino Brdo, no. **33**: *Ael(ius) Bessus et | Ael(ia) Ursa fil(iae).* For Katičić (MDN 264) *Bessus,* together with *Besius,* belongs to the middle Dalmatian onomastic group. Besssus appears in the inscriptions in Dalmatia, Dacia, Moesia Superior, Bessula, from the same root Bes-. is attested in Gallia Belgica, Pannonia and Gallia Narbonensis;[114] Bessio is known in Kolovrat near Prijepolje, *Statio Bessioni et Annae Severinae,* Cermanović-Kuzmanović, Istorijski arhiv, Titovo Užice 1989, 7, no. 4.

Bessus could be the name-ethnic, like *Dardanus, Delmana* or *Narensis* in the inscriptions from Kolovrat. Bessi were the Thracian tribe, but they are recorded in Appian, Illyr.16 also as one of the people which Octavian defeated in his Illyrian war in BC. 35-33. There is ground to suppose that the tribe Bessi lived also in the later province of Dalmatia.

One *Aurelia Vendo* appears again on the monuments found on Ilijino Brdo, no. **27**: *D(s) M)anibus) S(acrum) | Aur(eliae) Vendoni | q(uae) v(ixit) a(nnis) XXIII T. Aur(elius) VS[ ].* Another Aurelia **Vendo** appears as the name of the veteran's wife in the inscription no. **17**. Her husband, the veteran Aurelius Maximus bears common soldiers name. He could be of native origin.

The husband of one **Vendo** in an inscription from Komini bears the native name *Plarens*:

49. Funerary slab of limestone height 126 width 72 thick 38 cm. In the upper part is represented gable with wrath and rose in the middle, both corner right and left of the gable are decorated by leaves and fruit. Discovered *in situ*, in the tomb I together with the monument no. ---. in the Necropolis II in 1966.

A. Cermanović-Kuzmanović, Starinar 18, 1967, no. 6. with photo and eadem, Hommage à Marcel Renard III, 1969, 119, with photo.

D(is) M(anibus) S(acrum) | Aurel(iae) | Veñdoni | q(uae) v(ixit) a(nnis) XXX ⁵| Âureĥus | Plaren|s c(oniugi) b(ene) m(erenti) | p(osuit).

Another *Aurelius* **Plarens** appears in another inscription from Pljevlja as the son of *T. Aurelius Severus Celsianus* who had a tomb in the necropolis II in Komini:

50. Funerary monument height 114 width 54 thick 54 cm. The inscription and both lateral sides are in the decorated frame. On both lateral sides is represented Athis with torch in his hand turned down. It have been fond in one of

---

[114] Lörincz, Onomasticon, s.v.

three tombs in the necropolis in the foot of the hill Bijeli Breg 1899 (tomb I) which have been excavated by the Austrian officers and transported in the garden of the military barracks in Pljevlje. Still in the same place, immured in the Alexander's well.

Patsch, WMBH 8, 1902, 117, no. 3 with photo fig. 54; CIL III 14605; Vulić, Spomenik 71, 1931, no. 283 and idem, Spomenik 98, 1041-48, 307, with photo of the front side and one of the lateral sides. Cf. photo by. A. Cermanović-Kuzmanović, Die antike Welt 1973, 2, 5, Fig. 4 and 5.

D(is) M(anibus) S(acrum) | T. Aûr(elio) Seve|ro Celsiâno | q(ui) v(ixit) an(nis) LXXX | Aur(elius) Plares | fil(ius) p(atri) p(ientissimo) p(osuit).

Plares appears in Kolovrat in the family in which all names are Illyrian, the wife is *Aurelia Scenuta* and children are *Lavius* and *Delmana*.[115] *Delmana* could be the name-ethnic which reminds on the Dalmatian origin. *Plares* witch has also the form *Plarens* is common name of Delmatae but appears also as in the group of south Illyrian names. The name is known in Stolac in Hercegovina, in Doclea and in the Dalmatian region, in Salona and Tilurium.[116] *Plarens*, the recipient of the military diploma CIL XVI 38 appears as *Deramista*.

All members in the family in the inscription no. **16** bear Illyrian names: the father was *Aurelius Aplis*, the mother *Aurelia Vendo* and the son was *Aurelius Turus*: *T. Aurel(io) Aplini | vetr(ano) (!) q(ui) v(ixit) a(nnis) LXX | et Aur(eliae) Vendoni | coniugi T.Aur(elius) Turus p(arentibus) p(iissimis) p(osuit).*

The name **Turus** appears in the Municipium also as feminin form **Turo**:

51. Funerary monument with the inscription which is published on the basis of the copy and photo made by certain Potparić, Vulić, Spomenik 71, 1931, p. 244, ad no. 287b. with photo.

D(is) M(anibus) Aurel(ia) | Turo | Pinsi f(ilia) | q(uae) v(ixit) [ ]

Mayer, Ill. Sprache 346 determine *Turus* as Illyrian name which was common in the west Dalmatia, for instance *Turo Statica Aplinis* f. in the inscription from Danilo, C. III 2797, *Aplo Darmoca Turi f*, from Rider. For Alföldy, PND 61 the name is of Liburno-Venetian origin. The name appears in the surrounding of Municipium, in Derikonjići near Prijepolje: *Aurelia Turoni [---]*, Vulić, Spomenik 71, 1931, no. 331, with photo (A. et J. Šašel. ILJug. 1696) recognize as *tubon*,. It must be either masculine form –o, or metronym witch didn't disappear in the central Balkan regions in the second and third century. In the quoted monument two male and one female busts are represented in the upper part. The feminine form *Turo* prevailed among known samples. *Turo* f. appears in the inscription from Karan near Užice.[117] **Turo** in Pljevlja and in Karan indicates probably the same origin of the people in both regions. One more sample bears the inscription no. **53**: *Catoni Statariae Tu[r]i.*

Pinsus belongs to the names which are common in Rider and Vrlike, once also connected with **Turus**: *Pinsus Germanicus Turi fil.,* Katičić. MDN 273.

52. The Illyrian name ***Brizidia*** appears on the altar of limestone dedicated to Iuppiter, height t 43 thick 29 cm. It was immured in the Mehmed aga Selatović's house, now in the yard of Steva Kovačević in Babiš Potok near Komini.

Patsch, WMBH IV, 42; CIL III 8302;Vulić, Spomenik 98, 1941-48, 130, no. 288, with photo.

I(ovi) O(ptimo) m(aximo) | Statius | Victor Bri|zidia v(otum) l(ibens) s(olvit).

Brizidia has in the position of the third name or second cognomen. Mayer, Ill. Sprache 97 brings only this sample and defines the name as Illyrian, as well as Alföldy PND, 166 with hesitation ('warscheinlich illyrisch'). The latter explains the name as the place name.

Cato is one of the Illyrian names which is frequent in the coastal zone before all. In the interior of the Dalmatia is known only in Bajina Bašta to day,[118] in Prijepolje and in Pljevlja:

53. Limestone slab. In the upper part in a gable is represented the wreath with the rose in the middle. In the corners right and left of the gable are represented dauphins. Discovered in Pljevlja, immured high in one tower:

Blau, Monatsbericht Acad. Berol. 1866, 849 (CIL III 6356); Hoernes, AEM 4, 1880, 189, no. 19 (CIL III 8323); Patsch, GZM 6, 1894, 472, no. 13, fig. 1 and WMBH 4, 280, no. 13 with drawing fig. 54 (CIL III 13846). Cf. Vulić, Spomenik 71, 1931, no. 291 (only the photo).

D(is) M(anibus) | Câtoni Stata|riae Tu(r?)i q(uae) v(ixit) an(nis) L | Q. Ael(ius) Stâtia|nus coñiu(gi) | b(ene) m(erenti) p(osuit).

The name appears as name of *Aplis Pantonis* wife's in Kolovrat near Prijepolje, Mirković, Godišnjak CBI 12, 1975, 98, no. 3. *Cato* could be also masculine form (Krahe PN 29: *Matta Catonis* (Pannonia Superior.) and *M.Caton Varo* from Iader. **Catta** with double *tt* is characteristic for the region of Bajina Bašta near Užice. (Katičić, MDN 266). Here is feminine form -o, with patronym.

---
[115] Cermanović-Kuzmanović, A new inscription from Kolovrat, Archaeologia Iugoslavica XIX, 1978, 46-48.
[116] G. Alföldy, BNF 15, 89 i 99.
[117] P. Petrović, Rimski kameni spomenici iz Karana, 1986, no. 8.
[118] Katičić, MDN, 266 (*Cato, Catta*).

Stataria should be one of the names which is determined as typical for the middle Dalmatian area.[119] The name is of Venetian origin (Alföldy PND with *Turo Statici Aplinis* from Rider).

Tui is probably to be completed in **Tu(r)i** as the inscription found near Salona proves: *Turoni Statariae Turi f.* Bull. Dalm. 34, 1911, p. 50, cf. Rendić –Miočević, Ilirska onomastika, 1948, 39, as the sample illustrating the onomastic formula name + "prezime" + *filius* Both, *Statianus* in the inscription from Pljevlja and *Statarius* in Salona could be related and derived from the same root.

Durus is native name of Cetic origin. It appears in municipium on the gravestone.

54. Funerary limestone monument, partly cracket in the middle, height 135 width 78 thick 39 cm. In the upper part in the profiled arch are represented three busts: female in the middle, smaller male on the right side and the of a child on the left. Female figure has a scarf on her head. In the corners left and right of the arch are represented ivy leaves. Discavered during the exavations of the Necropolis II in Komini in 1966.

A. Cermanović-Kuzmanović, Zbornik Filozofskog fakultetata XI-1, 1970, 75, no. 7 with photo. 7 (A. et J. Šašel, ILJug 608).

D(is) M(anibus) s(acrum) | Gav(ius) Dûr| us V̂aleria|no q(ui) v(ixit) [ ]

Gavius is frequent name in Dalmatia (Alföldy, PND), s.v., in Italy and in the western provinces (Lörincz, Onomasticon).

Durus could be Celtic name, deriving from the same root as *Durio, Durius, Duris* and as the geographic names *Durocatelaun, Durotrigus* (Holder, s.v.), *Durrius* appears in Pannonia, *Durrus* in the Gallia Belgica (Lörincz, s.v.).

Germanus is defined as Illyrian name. In the Pljevlja region appears on the monument found on the hill Ilijino Brdo, no. **20**.

Germanus, as well as the names *Germanicus, Germullus, Germus* and *Germaniscus*, appears in the inscriptions in the middle Dalmatian region, on in Rider, Alvona, Salona and Corfinium.[120]

Lavius is attested in the same inscription as **Tito**, both Illyrian, with the imperial gentile names Aurelius or Aelius. In Municipium it appears on the altar found in the Necropolis II:

55. Altar of limestone slightly damaged on the upper left side, height 135 wight 31.5 thick 76.5 cm. Letters height 5.5 cm. Found during the archaeological excavations by A. Cermanović-Kuzmanović, Starinar 32, 1982, 77 no. 5 with photo.

I(ovi) O(ptimo) M(aximo) C(ohortali) | Aur(elius) Lavius | et Ael(ius) Tito | l(ibentes) p(osuerunt)

Lavius, as well as *Lavus, Lavianus* and *Lavo*, is known in the inscriptions in the region Pljevlja and Prijepolje. It is considered typical for the Dalmatian nomenclature (Alföldy, PND 228; Mayer, Ill. Sprache 163). In Kolovrat, not far from Pljevlja, Lavius was *d(ecurio) m(municipii)*. He was of native origin as it is shown by other names in the inscription: his grand-father was *G. Suricinus*, his mother *Aurelia Madita*, and his sister was *Aur. Venuco*[121] all with epichoric names. His grandmother and his father bear Roman names *Sep(timia) Candida*, and *Aur. Maximus*. *Lavius* in the inscription from Djurovo near Prijepolje was *II vir* (A. et J. Šašel, ILJug. 75 a). Further sample from Kolovrat concerns *Statia Lavo* who erected the monument for her grand-son (*nepoti*) Valerius Optatus.[122] The samples from Rider (Katičić, MDN 271) allow to define the name as delmatian. Samples in Alburnus Maior in Dacia could be explained as belonging to the Illyrian who have been transported to the Dacian mines.

Tito and **Titus** are the names of the Illyrian origin. Titus appears in the inscription from Komini as *Titus PR.R.*:

56. Funerary slab height 150 width 59 thick 15 cm. In the upper part is represented female bust with the scarf on her head in the triangle gable.

A. Cermanović-Kuzmanović, Hommage à Marcel Renard III, 1969, 118 with photo Taf. XXXIX, Abb.1 (A. et J. Šašel, ILJug 610)

D(is) M(anibus) S(acrum) | Pâûl(ae?) Gau|deñe (!) q(uae) v(ixit) | ân(nis) XL Ti|tus PR.R. | coñp(ari) p(ientissimae) êt | sib(i) vîvo | p(osuit).

PAVL could be completed in *Paulia ili Paulla*. Seldom attested Greek name *Gaudene* (Lörincz, Onomasticon, notes only this example) could point to the servile condition.

Titus is frequent name in Prijepolje, in Kolovrat and other places in the Lim valley. It appears in different position in the nomeclature formula, once as the only name of the person (Cermanović-Kuzmanović, Užički zbornik 18, 1989, 5, no. 3), or as praenomen in the two names formula, *Titus [ ]atius*, on the monument from Radoinja, Bojanovski, Godišnjak CBI 23, 1987, 147. The position of praenomen *Titus* appears also in the three-names formula, *Titus Anae Codalianus* in the inscription from Kolovrat, Spomenik 98, 1941-1948, 333 and in one another from Džurovo near Prijepolje, *Titus Aelius Lavianus*, Starinar 1, 1950, 183-184. The onomastic formula *Titus Pr.P* in the inscription from Komini is

---

[119] Katičić, MDN 276, cf also Mayer, Illyr. Sprache, 322 with samples from Pljevlja and from Siculi near Salona in Dalmatia.
[120] Katičić, MDN 270.

[121] Garašanin, Istorija Crne Gore 1967, 225-228 (Mirković, Godišnjak CBI 1, 1975, 99, no. 5).
[122] Mirković, Godišnjak CBI 12, 100, no. 8.

enigmatic and unusual as well as the wife's name Paulla Gaudene. Abbreviation PR. could be completed in *Priscius, Priscinus* and similar. or *Primus* (Šašel), the letter *R*. which follows could represent the second cognomen in abbreviated form. If so, the person had three names, as *Titus Aelius Lavianus* or *Titus Annae Codalianus*. Less probable seems to bee the reading *pr(inceps) R.*

Probably Celtic name **Maxillo** (?), appears in the partly erased inscription from the cemetery I in Komini.

57. Funerary slab height 120 width 87 thick 34 cm. In the upper part represented gable with rose in the middle. Inscribed field in the profiled frame, letters height 5.5 to 6 cm. Damaged inscribed field.

Discovered during the archaeological excavations 1972 in the sonde IX, in the eastern part of the Necropolis I (Cermanović, ms. diary from the excavations 1972). Preserved in Komini.

```
D M S
M.A.XIL. L (?).O
V.AN XX
M.VLP   VS
CONIVGI
P P
```

Line 2: MAXI IITO Cermanović-Kumanović. ms. preserved in the Archaeological Collection at the Filofofski fakultet in Beograd

Possible reconstruction of the text:

D(is) M(anibus) s(acrum) | Maxillo | v(ixit) an(nis) XX | M. Ulp(ius) [..]us | coniugi | p(iissimae) p(osuit).

The name *Maxillo* could be related to *Maxa* which is attested in the country of Japodi, in the Una valley (CIL III 14015) witch Alföldy, BNF 15, 62 has considered as Celtic name (see Holder II 480: *Max-o, Max-acae*, and similar; names from the root MAXI are frequent in Italy and in the provinces, in Dacia and Britain.[123]

The name **Nantius** is attested on the gravestone discovered at Komini in 1975:

58. Limestione funerary slab height 145 width 70 (75) thick 20 cm. Letters height 6 and 5 cm. Discovered in the Necropolis II in Komini during the excavation not far from the grave 25/1975 with the ashes of the dead in the ceramic urne.

A. Cermanović-Kuzmanović, Starinar 32, 1982, 75, no. 1.

D(is) M(anibus) s(acrum) | Fl(aviae) Mar|cellae q(uae) v(ixit) | a(nnis) XXXIV | Nantius | Sexti c(oniugi) b(ene) m(erenti) p(osuit)

Nantius could be Illyrian or Celtic name. Alföldy, BNF 62, defined it as typical for the Japodes, and probably Celtic, Holder II 684, Alföldy PND 250). In Rider is attested *Nantanius. Cognatio Nantania* appears in an altar from Varvaria which was dedicated by Turus Longini f.[124] *Nantius* and similar is frequent not only in Dalmatia but also in Italy and in the provinces.[125]

Female name **Panto** is one of the most frequent in the inscriptions from Komini and Pljevlja. It appears as only one name or with the gentile name Aurelius. *Aurelia Panto* was buried in the family tomb of *Paconii*, one of the most prominent families in the city. She was married to Lucius Paconius Barbario and was mother of Paconia Montana R. and Paconius Barbarus, who was the city *decurio*.[126]

Aurelia Panto appears once again on the funerary monument from Pljevlje:

59. Funerary monument of limestone. In the upper part gable with the wreath in the middle, left and right a bird, and in the corners dauphins.

Evans, Antiquarian researches, 28, fig. 9; Patsch, WMBH 4, 1896, 283, no. 24; CIL III 8317; Vulić, Spomenik 98, 1941-48, no. 304, using the photo by D. Sergejevski.

D(is) M(anibus) S(acrum) | Aureliae | Pantoni | q(uae) v(ixit) a(nnis) XXXV | T.Aurelius Quintus | c(oniugi) b(ene) m(erenti) p(osuit)

Panto as the only name appears also on two other monuments:

60. Funerary slab of limestone broken in many fragments which fit one to another, height 110, width 86, thick 44 cm. In the upper part a gable with the rose in the middle.

Patsch, WMBH 12, 1912, 122-123, no. 6, with drawing.

D(is) M(anibus) S(acrum) | T. Aurel(io) In|genuo | q(ui) v(ixit) an(nis) L | et Pantoni coni(ugi) | ei(us) q(uae) v(ixit) an(nis) XXXV | T. Aurel(ius) Maxi|[m]us filius | [p(arentibus) p(ientissimis) p(osuit).

61. Fragment of the funerary slab of limestone. Upper part on the right side and lower part are lost. Height 50 width 38 thick 13 cm. In the upper part gable with the rose in the middle, right and left in the corners ivy leaves. Discovered in Necropolis II in Komini as one in the range of twelve funerary monuments following one another in the row, during the excavations 1967.

Cermanović-Kuzmanović, Starinar 18, 1967, no. 7 and eadem, Hommage à Marcel Renard, p. 119.

D(is) M(anibus) [s(acrum)] | Panton[i   ] |[...]AN ? Pant[ ]

---

[123] CIL III 1531, AE 1971, 370, AE 191867, 265, *Maxa, Maxentia*, in Dalmatia, Alfoldy, PND 241, see also ILJug 823, CIL III 3051, 12752 and 14321[24]. Cf. Lörincz III 68. For **Maxillo**, see Lörincz, Onomasticon, 2 with samples from Spain (Ameida 133, AE 1967, 265).

[124] Rendić-Miočević, ŽA 10, 1960, 165 ff. Cf. G. Alföldy, Acta ant. Hung. 11, 1963, 81 ff.
[125] Lörincz, Onomasticon, s.v.
[126] On *Paconii* in Municipium S( ) see below, p. 55 ff.

Line 3:]c Cerm.- Kuzm.

The name *Panto* is attested also in the inscriptions found in the surroundings of Municipium. In the village Podpeć to day is discovered the nomument no. **37**. The damaged name is completed in *Tes]toni* by A. Evans.

Aelia Panto is the wife of the local praefectus *Aelius Pladomenus Carvanio* in the inscription from Džurovo, no. **1b**. The name is frequnet in the region inhabited by the Delmatae, before all in Rider (7 from 15 samples known in 1963),[127] but also in other places (Salona, Aquileia). For Alföldy it is typical Dalmatian name.[128]

Pletor appears as the only name of the man on the newly discovered monument in Otilovići, about sex km on the East from Pljevlja, no. **40**.

Scaevianus appears once, on the the monument.

62. Funerary slab of limestone. In the upper part represented gable with wreath and rose in the middle. It was discovered in the ruions of mosque in Pljevlja (Vulić).

Patsch, WMBH 4, 1894, 280, no. 12 with drawing; CIL III 8313; Vulić, Spomenik 71, 1931, no. 291 (only photo) and Spomenik 98, 1941-48, 137, no. 302 with photo.

D(s) M(anibus) S(acrum) | T.Aelio Scae|viano q(ui) v(ixit) | a(nnis) LXX Ae|lii Titia|nus et Ae|lianus f(ilii) p(atri) | p(ientissimo) p(osuerunt)

Scaevianus is the name characteristic for the middle Dalmatian region. *Scaeva* is attested in the inscription from Župča near Visoko, *Scaevianus* is the name of the fleet soldier in Brundisium.[129]

The Illyrian name **Tata** (Mayer, Illyr. Sprache 330, with samples from Vrlike and Virunum) appears in the inscription from Pljevlja.

63. Fragment (right half) of the funerary slab of dark blue limestone height 160, width 41, thick 64 cm. The inscribed field in the rich decorated frame. In the frame on the right lateral side represented Atis with torch in his right hand. Found in Pljevlja in 1940 in the ruins of the mosque near the City house, thereafter in the yard of the Velika džamija (Big Mosque) where it was seen by Vulić.

Vulić, Spomenik 98, 1941-1948, no. 303 with unclear photo made by D. Sergejevski (A. et J. Šašel, ILJug 1712).

[D(is) M(anibus)] s(acrum) | [. Au]rel(ius) | [si]|[bi et? A]ure|[liae T]atae | [vi]vae | [...]sq(ve?) | [vi]v(us) p(osuit).

The name *Tata* or similar could be recognized in the badly damaged probably funeral inscription preserved in the notebook of A. Cermanović-Kuzmanović and as photo (Archaeological collection at the Filozofski fakultet Beograd).

64. Funerary? slab, marked as stele no. 25 in notbook by A. Cermanovic-Kuzmanović, was found in the Necropolis II on the outside of the tomb V during the archaeological excavations 1966 or 1967. In the hollowed field the damaged inscription in five lines:

M S
TATE
....
TA.....
AN

The Illyrian name **Testo** (Mayer, Illyr. Sprache, 334) appears with the gentile name *Aurelius* in the inscription found on Ilijino Brdo no. **22** (*Testoni*). It is considered the middle Dalmatian.[130] The masculine form *Testa* (Septimius) appears in the inscription in Ravna (Timacum Minus), far from the middle Dalmatian area, in the East of the province Upper Moesia.[131]

Titto appears among names on the Ilijino Brdo, no. **25**. Another name in the same inscription is partly erased *Cami[a?* or *Camb[rianus]*. It could be also Illyrian.

As *Tito* the name is known from an altar found in Kolovrat Cermanović-Kuzanović, Srarinar XXXII, 1981, 77, no. 5. Both *Titto* and *Tito* are Illyrian female names.[132] Alföldy PND 312 notes that the name is frequent in southern Gallia as masculine name, for instance in CIL XII 95.

Titianus, no. **4**, must have derived from Titus.

Tritano (Aurelia) is attested in the inscription from Ilijino Brdo, no. **26**. It is considered Illyrian by Mayer, 344, D. Rendić-Miočević, Iliri i antički svijet, 790 quotes many new samples: *Aplini Tritanonis*, Vrlika, *Tritano Curbania Triti f.*, Danilo. For Alföldy, BNF 84 the name is known in the region inhabited by Japodes, but also in Liburnia. *Tritus* is also frequent (nine samples in Rider). Katičič. MDN 278 included in the same group the names *Tritanus, Tritano and Tritaneria*.

The name **Verzo** or **Verzaio** could be recognized on a fragment found in the Necropolis I at Komini,

65. Small fragment of the funerary slab of the limestone, height 12 width 95? (or 10 and 19 cm in another place) thick 2 cm. Letters height 4 cm. Lines between double lines. Found in the quadrant III in the eastern, chronologically the latest part of the Necropolis I at Komini during the excavations 1972.

A. Cermanović-Kuzmanovič, ms. in the Archeological collection at the Filozofski fakultet Beograd.

---

[127] Katičić, MDN 272.
[128] PND 259, BNF 15, 1964, 83 and 100; Mayer, Ill. Sprache, 257.
[129] Katičić MDN 274.
[130] Katičić, MDN 277.
[131] p. Petrović, IMS III-2, no. 60.
[132] Mayer, Ill. Sprache 340.

NIS
R? VERZ

Illyrian name is *Verzo* and *Verzalio*.[133] The name is frequent in Alburnus Maior in Dacia: *Lavius Verzonis*, CIL III 1269, *Platinonis Verz[o]nis*, 1271, *Dasius Verzonis Pirusta ex Kavieretio Plani Verzonis Sclaetis*, CIL III cer.6. *Dasius Verzonis*, CIL III cer.17. The name could be treated as belonging to the pre-Roman native people on the wide territory which is determined as south-Illyrian and middle Illyrian. To this group belonged the Pirustae and the name came to Dacia when the Romans transported Pirustae to this province after Trajan's victory to work in the mines.[134]

Native names appear not only in the Municipium and its territory but also in the large area around Pljevlja. The only great concentration of inscriptions in which appear natives is in Kolovrat near Prijepolje, the place where Evans and others saw ruins of a big Roman settlement and on the hill Ilijino Brdo 5 km on the south of Pljevlja. Find spots of the Roman inscriptions are dispersed between them and far on the west and south, near Ivangrad and Nova Varoš. This area is relatively isolated and the survival of the native tribes or rest of them is to be expected. The majority of the names are Illyrian, some of them unknown out of this region The pre-Roman inhabitants in the Lim and Ćehotina valley left no certain trace in archaeological material; on the other hand there is no certain written evidence about the natives in the interior of the Roman province of Dalmatia and therefore is impossible to define them nearly. They could belong to the pre-Roman inhabitants of the region or to the immigrants.

Connection between the buried persons and the relationship between Romans and natives reveal the archaeological investigation made by A. Cermanović-Kuzmanović in the cemeteries in Komini. Topography of the graves and tombs of those bearing Roman or Illyrian names in the Necropolis II shows that both, Romans and natives were not separated in different parts of the cemetery but buried side by side.

Fig. 23: Fragment of the gravestone from Ivangrad

---

[133] Mayer, Ill. Sprache, 358. Katičić SIN, 110, quotes two samples from Montenegro (Grahovo: *Verzo*, JÖAI 12, 1909, Beibl. 202 and Berane (Budimlje near Ivangrad): *Aur. Verzaio liberto*, CIL III 13832 and one from Salone (*Titiae Verzonis f.*, CIL III 9056).

[134] For *Verzalio* in Budimlje near Ivangrad see CIL III 13832; Vulić, Spomenik 71, 1931, no. 11 with photo (A. et J. Šašel, ILJug. 1814).

IV. CEMETERIES, GRAVES AND FAMILIES IN THE ROMAN MUNICIPIUM

Citizens of the municipium were buried in two cemeteries both in use from the first to the fourth century. Both were archaeologically investigated in 1966-1967 and again in 1972-1973.[135]

The beginning of the burial in the older, necropolis I, was dated by A. Cermanović-Kuzmanović at the end of the first century BC or the beginning of the first century. It seems that the sepultures in necropolis I did not stop when the burial in necropolis II began. A total of three hundred and eighteen graves were discovered there with incinerated dead and only a few, mostly fragmented, funerary monuments with inscriptions. Only one funerary monument is completely preserved, but the inscription has been erased because of the humidity. The incinerated dead were buried in ceramic urns and small stone chests. The burials in this necropolis were performed without any fixed order. The first ones took place towards the end of the first century BC. The following fragments are discovered during the excavations:

Fig. 24: Necropolis I at Komini

66. Funerary slab discovered in 1972. in the necropolis I quadrant III. The inscribed field in the profiled frame.

Preserved in the notebook of the archaeological investigation by A. Cermanović-Kuzmanović (ms. in the Archaeological Collection at the Filozofski fakultet Beograd). Noted as the slab no. 25. Lost.

D M S
V I C O A I
 S S
AN. L. I ..
R COAI
NI CON
POS

It is possible to recognize only *D(is) M(anibus) S(acrum)* in line 1 and *con(iugi) pos(uit)* in lines 6-7.

67. Fragment of the limestone slab, heights 21 width 23 thick 55 cm (or 21 x 26 x 5.5 cm, in another note). Letters 4 and 3.5 cm. A. Cermanović-Kuzmanović suggested that it was secondary used to cover a small stone chest. Discovered in the necropolis I in the quadrant III during the excavations 1972.

Noted by A. Cermanović-Kuzmanović as the slab no. 24 (ms. Archaeological collection at the Filozofski fakultet Beograd).

uxo[ri
]avis anno.

68. A small fragment of the limestone height 12 width 17 cm (or 10 x 19 cm., in another note). Letters 4 cm. Found in the quadrant III during the excavations 1972.

NIS
R ? VERZ

The name in the line 2 could be completed in *Verzalio*.

The gravestone no. **57** with the inscription of Maxillo is also discovered also in the Necropolis I.

---
[135] Detailed study about necropolis I and II and the objects found in every grave prepares Mira Ružić, (Necropolises I and II in Municipium S.).

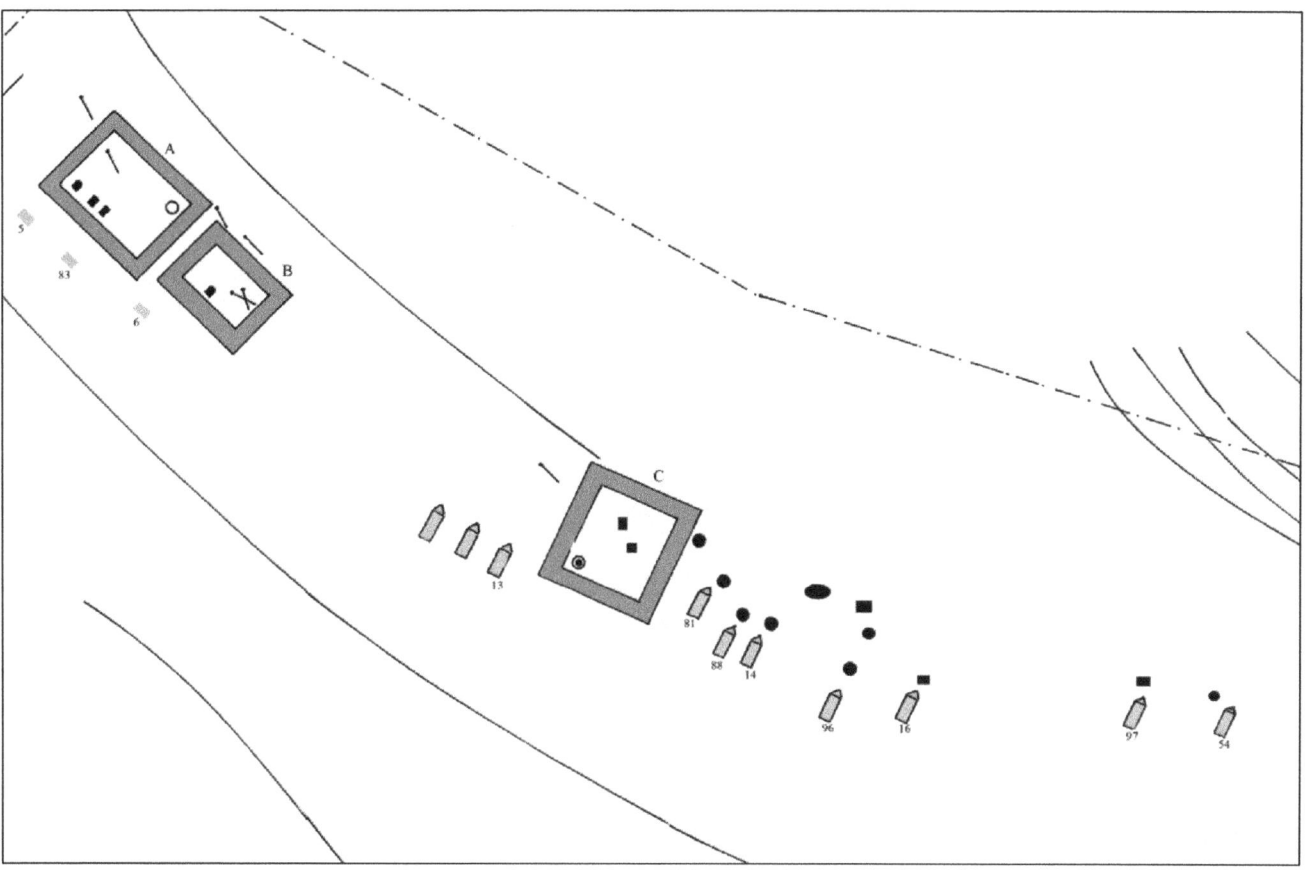

Fig. 25: Central part of the necropolis II at Komini (reconstructed by Mira Ružić)

Fig. 26: Necropolis II at Komini

Necropolis II was discovered on the slopes and in the plains in the foothills of Bijeli Brijeg. The burials here took place from the first to the fourth century. Two hundred and eighty two graves and eight family tombs have been discovered. They followed one another in several rows following the direction North – South on the natural terraces in the hill. The burials were performed in the same way as in Necropolis I, in ceramic urns or small stone chests. Some skeletons were buried directly in the earth in the 4th century. Many funerary monuments with inscriptions were found in the northern part of the cemetery *in situ*. All of them could be connected with some of the discovered graves. Fifteen graves with funerary monuments have been discovered. Eight family tombs contain several graves and funeral slabs bearing inscriptions. In the row from the North to the South the tombs and graves run as follows: tomb VIII, tomb VI, tomb V, the grave and funerary slab of Tata, the grave and funerary slab of Claudia Procula, tomb IV, a grave and gravestone slab decorated with ascia in the gable without inscription, tomb VII, the grave and funerary slab of Aurelia Vendo, the grave and funerary slab of Titus Aurelius Aplis, the grave and funerary slab of Ratonia Autumna, the grave and funerary slab of Paula Gaudene, the grave and funerary slab of Durus Valerianus, the grave and funerary slab of Septimus and Pilia, the grave and funerary slab of Marcus Fulvius Natalis, the grave and funerary slab of Aurelia Vendo, the grave and funerary slab of Statia, the grave and funerary slab of Lucius Paris, tomb III, the grave and funerary slab of Aulus Gablius, the tomb of Aurelia Maximina (n. I), and the tomb of Paconia Montana.[136]

PROMINENT FAMILIES

The name *Aurelius/ -a* appears with considerable frequency in the funerary monuments. Many of them bear also native, mostly Illyrian names. Only a few of the persons on the monuments were related by kinship.

---

[136] D. Srejović, Grobnice Aurelije Maksimine i Pakonije Montane u Kominima (Municipium S.), Zbornik Narodnog muzeja 8, Beograd 1975, 177-187.

Paconii, Lurii and *Cipii* were related, as is directly proved in inscription n. **78**. However, the monument relating to *Paconii, Cipii* and *Lurii* was not discovered in the part of the cemetery where the rest of *Paconii* had their tomb. The latter belonged to the newest part of the cemetery. It could be suggested two generations.

Aemilii, Arg(eniani), or similar), *Egnatii, Paconii* and *Statii* belonged to the group of families who played an important role in the municipium. They appear in many monuments and had a family tomb in Necropolis II.

Aemilii

They must have been very important in the city administration. *Aemilii* are attested among the city magistrates. M.Aemilius Antonius was *II vir* in the city (no. 3), Aemilius Titianus was II *vir quinquennalis* (no. 4). The name appears many times on altars: no. 3 dedicated to Iuppiter Fulgurator, no. 4 to Iuppiter Optimus Maximus; the third was dedicated to Iuppiter Cohortalis (no. 69) fourth to Silvanus (no. 70); fifth is the gravestone (no. 71).

69. Limestone altar: height 80, width 46, thick 39 cm. In the upper part is represented a rose. It was found in the house of Hadži-aga Popović in Pljevlje, immured on the right side of the house entrance.

Hoernes, AEM 4, 1880, 191, no. 1; CIL III 8299; Patsch, GMBH 6, 1894, 477 and WMBH 4, 1898, 284, no. 25; Sergejevski, Spomenik 98, 1941-48, 145.

   I(ovi) C(o)hor(tali) | s(acrum) | M. Aemil(ius) Antonius v(otum) l(ibens) p(osuit).

70. Limestone altar height 90, width 56, thick 45 cm. Discovered on the banks of the small river Vezičnice, transported to the barracks in Pljevlje and immured in the steps in the garden.

Evans, Archaeologia XLIX, 1885, 31; Patsch, WMBH IV, 1896, 277, no. 1; CIL III 8306; Vulić, Spomenik 98, 1941-48, no. 296, with photo made by D. Sergejevski.

   Silvano | Aug(usto) sac(rum) | M.Aemiliu[s] | Anto[nius] | v(otum) s(olvit) [l(ibens) m(erito)].

Aemilius Calvinus, a relative of the city magistrates, was buried in Salona. His cenotaph was located in the municipium:

71. Funerary slab damaged at the top and lower part: height 92, width 75, thick 23 cm. Described by local teacher Vas. Marković as, 'richly decorated in the upper part'. It was immured in the steps of the Murad-beg Selmanović's house in Pljevlje.

Vulić, Spomenik 71, 1933, 119, no. 288.

   D(is) M(anibus) s(acrum) | Aemilii An|tonius et | Antoninus ⁵| Aemilio Calvi|ni def(uncto) Salo|[nis   ]

Lines 5/6: *Calvio|ni* Vulić, following the copy made by Vas. Marković.

Argeniani or similar

Aurelius Maximus Argenianus, whose tomb was discovered in the newest part of necropolis II in Komini (no. 6), also belonged as *decurio municipii* to the upper class which governed the city.

Sex. Aurelius Arg( ), n. **45** could have originated from the same family. The abbreviation *Ar* could be completed as *Argenianus, Argurianus* or *Argurinus*.

Arguriani and Argurinii

Arguriana was the second cognomen of *Aurelia Titulla*, no. **46**. Her aunt (*amita*) on her father's side was Aurelia Titula Cambria. The latter could be linked with *Cambrianus* on monument no. **47**. *Argurinus* appears as the second cognomen on monument no. **48** with the Illyrian name *Aplis Aureli Argurinus*.

Argurianus, Argurinus and similar could have been of native origin.

Egnatii

The name Egnatius appears on two monuments from the municipium. The Greek cognomen of his wife in the first and of Egnatia who was married to Gavius on the second inscription indicate the connection with the hellenophone group of people of Greek or oriental origin. Both monuments belong to the same period of time. Typologically they belong together.

72. Limestone funerary monument: height 161, width 72, thick 21 cm. Gable on the upper part; inscribed field in the profiled frame.

Patsch, WMBH 12, 1912, 126. no. 10 with drawing.

   D(is) M(anibus) | Caesi|ae Asêri|di q(uae) v(ixit) a(nnis) XXXV | C.Egnati|us Monta|nus c(oniugi) b(ene) m(erenti) | p(osuit).

Egnatia Soteris in another inscription originated probably from the same family. She married *Publius Gavienus Candidianus*.

73. Funerary slab damaged at the top: height 58, width 95, thick 33 cm. Gable on the upper part; inscribed field in the profiled frame.

Patsch, WMBH 12, 1912, 125, 9. 9, with drawing fig. 51.

   D(is) M(anibus) s(acrum) | P. Gavieno | Candidiano | q(ui) v(ixit) a(nnis) XLV et Egna|tiae So[te]r[i]di c[o]niugi | vivâê Gâv[i]en[i] Vale|riañus et Egna[ti]us êt | Candida filii p(arentibus) p(osuerunt).

Only a few Greek names are attested in the inscriptions from the municipium. In addition to its appearance in the

Egnatii family, the Greek name *Asclepiades* also appears in the *Statii* family who originated from Risinium (no. **79**), and *Paris* on the monument which was found in necropolis II:

74. Two fragments of a funerary slab height 94, width 75, thick 17 cm. The stone crumbled when it was excavated. It was found in necropolis II in 1965 close to grave no. 4 with ceramic urns.

A. Cermanović-Kuzmanović, Zbornik Filozofskog fakulteta XI-1, 1970, 75, no. 1 with photo fig. 1:

[D(is)] M(anibus) | [   ] n sibi et L[   ] | [   ]cio Pâridî | [   ] coniugi b(ene) [m(erenti) p(osuit)].

Text reconstructed by Cermanović-Kuzmanović.

Gavii or *Gavieni*

Probably the same family to which *Durus* belonged (no. **54**) where the name is abbreviated as *Gav( )*. *Durus* could be a Celtic name. Gavienus appears in inscription no. **54**.

Both forms, *Gavius* and *Gavinenus* are very frequent. *Gavii* were a known family in Aquileia.[137]

Paconii

Paconii were one of the most prominent families in the society of the Roman city. *Paconius Barbarus*, in inscription no. **5**, was elected *decurio* in the municipium. The members of the family are recorded on five monuments in the municipium. Three of them were found in necropolis II in Komini during the excavations, two were discovered as secondary used as building material and immured in the Turkish mosque and in a house in Pljevlje. The first two were discovered in tomb II and could be linked with the graves in it; one *Paconius* appears on the monument of *Furii* in the older part of the necropolis. They probably did not belong to the same generation. They are connected not only by the gentile name Paconius, but also by their cognomen. The cognomen *Barbarus* or *Barbarius* was common and probably inherited in the family.

The monumental tomb II in which *Paconius Barbarus*, his wife *Aurelia* with the Illyrian name *Panto*, their son *Paconius Barbar( )*, *decurio municipii* (no. **5**) and her daughter *Paconia Montana* (no. **75**) were buried was constructed at some distance from the other tombs and graves in Necropolis II. Two monuments which were found in Pljevlje could not be linked with this tomb, close to which no graves have been found in the archaeological investigations. The municipal decurio, mentioned in inscription no. **5** was buried in one of the graves in tomb II:

D(is) M(anibus) S(acrum) | L. P(aconio) Barbaro | d(ecurioni) m(unicipii) ? R. q(ui) vî(xit) ânni(s) | X̂X m(nsibus) III d(iebus) IIII L. P(aconius) Barbar( ) | êt Âur(elia) Pantô | filio incôn|parabili êt | sibi vivî in|felicisimi (!) | p(osuerunt)

Another monument which was discovered in the same tomb was dedicated to the memory of *Paconia Montana R.* It was erected by her mother *Aurelia Panto G.*

75. Funerary monument in the form of a large rectangular stone block of limestone height 29, width 63, thick 55 cm. In the aedicule on the right lateral side under the arch there is a nude male figure with a small wing on his right shoulder and a basket full of grapes on the left. The figure is holding a grape and the knife which was used in the vineyards in his right hand, and he is wearing boots on his feet. On the left lateral side of the monument in a similar aedicule there is a female figure wearing a long dress and shoes, with two flowers in her right hand and a key in her left. Her hair is parted in the middle.

The inscribed field on the front is in a profiled frame decorated by a vine with grapes which is tied in the Hercules knot on the top of the monument. Found in necropolis II, in the enclosed part of tomb II with two small stone chests for ashes.

A. Cermanović-Kuzmanović, Hommage à Marcel Renard III, 1969, 118 with photo and eadem, Starinar 18, 1967, 202, no. 2 with photo (A. et J. Šašel, ILJug.609).

D(is) M(anibus) S(acrum) | Pac(oniae) Mon|tanâe R. q(ui) | vî(xit) a(nnis) X̂X̂X̂V Âur(elia) | Panto G. | mât(er) fîlîe (!) dulcisîme (!) | êt s(ibi) vive (!) in|felicisîme (!) | p(osuit).

The letters *R* in the name of Paconia Montana and *G* in the name of her mother Aurelia Panto were probably an abbreviated form of the father's clan. The letter R also appears in the name of the son Paconius in inscription no. **5**.

Only the mother took care of the erection of the monument, the same *Aurelia Panto* as in monument **5**. The father probably died in the meantime.

The monuments in tomb II, n. **5** and **75** have much in common. They belong typologically to the same group of large quadrangular stone blocks with inscriptions on the front side and elaborated lateral sides, with human figures. The inscribed field is in a richly decorated frame, as on monument **75**.

Two monuments which were found immured in the later buildings in Pljevlje resemble one another, but differ sharply from the aforementioned, both typologically and in terms of elaborations. Both are funerary slabs, made to stand as the terrestrial mark on the individual grave, not in the tomb. They have a gable decorated with a rose and wreath on the upper part and palm leaves on both sides; the inscribed field is in a simple frame.

---
[137] Lörincz, Onomasticon s.v.

Fig. 27: The funeral monument of Paconia Montana (Is 75a, 75b and 75c)

Fig 28: Portraits of the male figure on the gravestone of Paconia Montana (lateral side)

Fig. 29: Male portrait on the fragment of the funeral monument found in the Necropolis II at Komini

Fig. 30: Lion – a part of the funerary monument in the Necropoilis II

76. Funerary slab broken in two: a) height 93, b) height 86 cm, width 74, thick 24 cm. On the upper part there is a gable decorated with a wreath with a rose in the middle. Found in Pljevlje.

Patsch, WMBH 12, 1912, 123, no. 7 with drawing fig. 49.

D(is) M(anibus) S(acrum) | L. Paconio | Barbarioni | q(ui) v(ixit) [a(nnis) X]XXL | [et...]uni | [c(oniugi) ei(us)] vivae | Val(erius) Fau|[s]tus p(arentibus) p(ientissimis) p(osuit).

The name Faustus appears again in the *Paconii* family (n. **85**). It is remarkable that the father (*Paconius*) and the son (*Valerius*) have different gentile name. As can be seen in the drawing, there was a place for the mother's family name, which could also have been Valeria.

77. Funerary slab: height 145, width 83.5, thick 31.5 cm. In the upper part the gable is decorated with a wreath with a rose in the middle.

Patsch, WMBH 12, 1912, 125 with drawing fig. 50.

D(is) M(anibus) S(acrum) | M.Pl( ) Ursino | q(ui) v(ixit) a(nnos) LV | L. Pac(onius) Barbar(io) | et Ursin[a] | b(ene) m(erenti) [p(osuit)]

The name in line 2 could be completed as Pl(etorius) or similar.

Paconii were also connected with other important families in the city. Paconius Barbar( ) appears as *cognatus* together with Luria Frunita on the funerary monument of Lucius Cipius Faustus and Frunita.

78. Limestone funerary slab: height 70, width 84, thick 20 (30) cm. The inscribed field is decorated on the left and right sides with ornamental 'fish bones'. Letters 6.9 to 3.9 cm. Discovered in necropolis Ii in the 1975 excavations.

A. Cermanović-Kuzmanović, Starinar XXXII, 1982, 75-76, no. 2.

D(is) M(anibus) s(acrum) | L. Cipio | Fausto êt | Fruñitâe | fil(iae) L. Pacoñi|us Barbario | cognâtus êt | Lûria Fruñita | frâtri êt ñepû | b(ene) m(erentibus) p(osuerunt)

Valerius, the son of L. Paconius Barbario, also bears the cognomen *Faustus* in inscription n. **76**.

The monument was erected in the tomb of *Cipii*. There is no indication that L. Paconius Barbaro as the *cognatus*, i.e the mother's relative, was buried in the same tomb. However, even between this monument and other Paconii monuments there are slight differences, in the first place in the paleography of inscriptions and details in the elaboration of the frames. The letters on monument nos. **5** and **75** are deeply incised, often in the ligatures and

Fig. 31: Funerary monument of L. Cipius Faustus (Necropolis II)

smaller in the last five lines. The letters on monuments **78** are longer, but not as deeply incised. All three are unlikely to belong to the same generation. *Paconii* on the monuments found in tomb II differ from *Paconius* on monument **78** as some of them have a second cognomen radically abbreviated to one letter, *R* or *G*. The name of the wife is Illyrian Panto. They could represent two different generations as the tomb of the latter was built in the oldest part of necropolis II.

Paconii are also known in the other part of the province of Dalmatia.[138]

Statii, Statiani, Startarii

Statii were buried in necropolis II at Komini. They seem to have belonged to the upper class in the municipium. The name *Statius*, frequent in Italy and the provinces, is also known in Dalmatia.[139] All *Statii* in the municipium are not likely to have been members of the same family.

---
[138] G. Alföldy. PND.
[139] Lőrincz, s.v.

Some of them came to the municipium from the coastal zone in Dalmatia. Statia Amoene originated from Risinium:

79. Funerary slab of crumbling limestone: height 160, width 75, thick 30 cm. Inscribed field in a profiled frame. Inscription badly damaged. Discovered in necropolis II in Komini during the archaeological investigations in 1965.

A. Cermanović-Kuzmanović, Zbornik Filozofskog fakulteta Beograd XI-1, 1970, 76, n. 2 with photo (A. et J. Šašel, ILJug 613).

D(is) M(anibus) | Statiae A|m?[.]enae [.] | [.]ISIN v(ixit) a(nnis) XL ^{5}| Co[...] Ascle|piades ? con|iugi [....]| Stat(ia) Ser?[.]en|sis matri f(ecit).

Line 2: *Am?[.]enae* Cerm.-Kuym., *Aspasiae* f. Šašel,

Line 3: |p [ ]ae[ ] Cerm.Kuzm.

Line 4: *[R]isin.* Šašel; *Risin* in the photo.

Lines 5/6: C[ ] *Ascle|p [co]n.* CO could be recognized on the photo as well as CO at the end of the line.

The completion *[R]isini* allows for the possibility that the deceased *Statia* originated from the costal zone in the southern part of the Roman province of Dalmatia. The mother could have originated from Senia in middle Dalmatia. Her second name could be completed as *Senensis.* Greek names appear as cognomen. The persons mentioned in this inscription were probably freedwomen of *Statii.*

Other *Statii* were closely connected with the natives in the municipium. Their connection with the natives is proved by names, as in no. 52. The second cognomen of *Statius Victor Brizidia* is Illyrian.[140] This was the family which differs from other *Statii* in the town.

Statia appears as the name of the daughter in the native family in Otilovići near Pljevlja, n. 40. The father *Pletor* is of Illyrian origin, without gentile name, mother is Maximina. The daughter is *Statia Fuscina*. Fuscina derives from Fusca which is attested in this region (Ana Fusca, no. **43** and in an inscription from Ilijino Brdo, no. **35**).

Sex. Statius Restitutus in inscription **22** from Ilijino Brdo is closely connected with the natives. His wife *Aurelia Testo* bears an Illyrian name.

Native names are also attested in the *Statii* family in the Roman settlement of Kolovrat near Prijepolje:

A. Cermanović-Kuzmanović, Užički zbornik 18, 1989, no. 4, with photo.

D(is) M(anibus) s(acrum) | C. Stat(io) Bes|sioni et A[n]^5|nae Severi|nae coi(ugi) eius | Stat(ius) Veloc[i]|anus et S[e]|verina p(ientissimis) p(osuerunt).

The name *Besssus* is attested in Dalmatia, Dacia and Moesia Superior. *Bessio* could have been an ethnic name as were Delmana and Narensis in the inscriptions from Prijepolje. If so, it concerns someone from the Thracian tribe *Bessi.* However, the names *Besius, Bessus, Bessula* are also known in the Celtic lands, Gallia Narbonensis and Lugdunensis and in Spain.[141]

In an inscription from Kolovrat *Stattius* appears with the Illyrian cognomen *Lavo*:

Mirković, Godišnjak 12, 1975, 100, no. 8, with photo.

D(is) M(anibus) | Val(erius) Optatu(s) | v(ixit) a(nnos) LXX Statia | Lavo v(iva) s(ibi) et P[.]|ae nep(oti) s(uae) q(uae) v(ixit) | an(nos) V.

THE REST OF THE CITIZENS WITH ROMAN NAMES

80. Fragment of the funerary monument. Preserved only the left upper corner with gable. Discovered at Komini.

Vulić, Spomenik 71, 1931, no. 286, with photo and idem, Spomenik 98, 1941-1948, no. 290 (A. et J. Šašel, ILJug. 1723)

Vulić: *D(is) M(anibus) [s(acrum)] | Q. Ael(ius) [Fau]st[us?...] | et [...],*

Line 3: St[...]Šašel.

81. Funerary slab height 68 width 45 thick 30 cm. Inscribed field in the frame decorated by vine with leaves and grapes. Found in Pljevlja on the Ćehotina river bank.

Hoernes, AEM 4, 1880, 192; CIL III 8316.

D(is) M(anibus) s(acrum) U[.]sinu[...] | Aur(elius) Ru[fus] | sibi et SV[..]| con(iugi) viv[us] t(itulum) f(aciendum) c(uravit).

82. Altar of limestone damaged on the upper part, height 51 width 33 thick 33 cm. Found in the ruins of the Roman town in Komini and transported in the military barracks in Pljevlja (Patsch).

Patsch, GMBH 6, 1894, 468, no. 2 and idem, WMBH IV, 1896, 277, no. 2; CIL III 12715 + p. 2255; Vulić, Spomenik 98, 1941-48, no. 297, with photo by D. Sergejevski. Cf. Vermasseren II 262, no. 1886; Lj. Zotović, Mitraizam na tlu Jugoslavije, 1973, no. 54 (A. et J. Šašel, ILJug. 1701).

---

[140] Mayer, Ill. Sprache, 97; Alföldy PND, 166 ('warscheinlich illyrisch'). He suggests but hesitantly the geographic meaning of the name.

[141] Lörincz, Onomasticon, s.v.

Soli In|victo sac(rum) | *Sext(us) Babe|rius I ânu⁵|[ar(ius)] v(otum) p(osuit) m(erito).*

Lines 4-5: IANV|AR VcI MI Patsch, IN|AR VoIM CIL III, *Ianu|[ar(ius) v(otum) p(osuit) m(erito)* Vulić.

Baberius is not a frequent name. Lörincz knows only this examples in the western provinces (Onomasticon, s.v.).

83. Two fragments of the funerary slab, height 87 width 67 thick 31 cm. Inscribed field in the profiled frame. Found in the necropolis II at Komini during the excavations in 1965.

A. Cermanović-Kuzmanović, Hommage à Marcel Renard II, 1969, 120 with photo Tab. XLI, abb. 3 (Šašel, ILJug. 606).

D(is) [M(anibus) S(acrum?)] | Claudi[ae] | Proculae | que (!) vixit an|nis XXVII Luc[i]|us Valens Or( ) | coniugi p(ientissimae) p(osuit).

OR in the line 5 could be the second cognomen in abbreviated form.

84. Altar of limestone height 41 width 24 thick 20 cm. In upper the part decorated with rose and leaves. Letters 2.5 cm.

Now in Museum in Pljevlja.

A. Cermanović-Kuzmanović, Starinar 32, 1982, 76-77, no. 4, with photo.

Ĥerculi | s(ancto) Cornif|icius Ve|rus l(ibens) v(oto) p(osuit)

85. Funerary slab of marble. In the upper part are represented two portraits in an aedicule. Inscribed field in the profiled frame.

Engelius, Geschichte der Freystaat Ragusa, p.133 (CIL III 1709); Blau, Monatsblatt Acad. Berol. 1866, p. 849; CIL III 6353; Hoernes, AEM 4, 1880, 189; Evans, Antiquarian researches, p. 26 with drawing; CIL III 8324; Patsch, GMBH 6, 1894, 10 and WMBH 4, 1896, 10.

D(is) M(anibus) s(acrum) | Dexter | êt Aṁa v̂îlis (!) | vi(vi) s(ibi) p(osuerunt) êt Ma|siṁîle fîlie (!) q(uae) vi(xit) an(nis) XXV.

Line 3: M Blau, M̂A Hoernes and Evans; line 6 *ex. XXV* Blau, *vi(xit) an(nis)* others.

86. Fragment of the funerary slab of limestone, height 66 width 58 thick 28 cm. Inscribed field in the profiled frame. Discovered in the archaeological excavations in the necropolis II at Komini 1974.

A. Cermanović-Kuzmanović, Starinar 32, 1982, 76, no. 3 with photo T. II.

Q. Valeño | Quadra|to an(norum) LXI | L. Val(erius) Ce Îêî [ ]

87. Lower part of the funerary slab height 120, wight 76, thick 15 cm. Found in the necropolis II in Komini 1965.

A. Cermanović-Kuzmanović, Zbornik Filozofskog fakulteta, Beograd XI-1, 1970, 77, no. 3 with photo fig. 3.

[ ] | ae ...]pat(ri) et Au|lae? [.] EPAE êt Sabi|no Certo ge|ñeñ êt M̂axiṁe ⁵| ñe<e>potâe M.Fûlvinus Na|talis b(ene) m(erenti) p(osuit).

Line 1: *ae Pa et Pau* Cerm.-Kuzm.

Line 2: *lae[ ]ae* Cerm.-Kuzm.

Line 5: NEEPOPAE Cerm-Kuzm. The letter E is in the ligature and again incised; the letter T seems to be certain.

88. Funerary slab of limestone 148 x 84 x 26 cm. Right upper corner is broken. In the upper part under an arch portraits of which only female on the left side is preserved. In the corner ivy leaves and a flower. Discovered during the excavations in 1965.

The inscription is erased and difficult to reconstruct.

A. Cermanović-Kuzmanović, Zbornik Filozofskog Fakulteta XI-1, 1970, 78, no. 5 with photo fig. 5.

D(is) M(anibus) S(acrum) | S[ ]PMÂ O V̂ or Q̂V̂ | [ ]NE q(uae) v(ixit) | a(nos) LXV C PI | LIE DESPO|tianus avi|ae p(ientissimae) et matri | viv(a)e et R( ) Pili|ae p(osuit), Cerm.-Kuzm.

It could run as follows:

D(is) M(anibus) [s(acrum)] | S[e]p[t]miâe Ôv[i]n?[...]ine q(ui) v(ixit) | an(nos) LXX Ĉepi|[ius] et Despo|tianus avi|âe p(ientissimae) êt matri ⁵| vive et R( ) fili|âe p(osuerunt).

89. Monument seen by Evans on the left bank of the river Ćehotina.

Patsch couldn't find it (WMBH 4,1896, 29).

Evans, Archaeologia XLIX (1885), 30; CIL III 8328.

```
//// //
///IAEO
VIXIT
XXXX
ILEVPIA
ONIVGI
MP
```

Line 5: *Aure]l(ia) Eup[l]ia*, CIL III, probably *Ulpia*, line 6 *coniugi* line 7 *m(emoriam) p(osuit)*.

90. Fragment of the funerary slab of limestone, discovered in 1964 in the necropolis II at Komini.

---] a(nis) XX | T.Au[r( )   ] | con(iugi)

*

In the necropolis II at Komini have been found fragments which were noted by A. Cermanović-Kuzmanović in her notebook during the excavations. Some of them could be linked with excavated graves.

91. Fragment of limestone. Unpublished.

D(is) M(anibus) | [...A]ur(elius) Ti[...] | [...]tur...| [...]P PI | ...

92. Upper part of the funerary monument in the form of a large square slab. Inscribed field in the profiled frame. Discovered in the necropolis II close to the tomb VIII 1967. Photo and note by A. Cermanović-Kuzmanović, ms. in the Archaeological collection at the Faculty of Philosophy in Beograd.

D(is) M(anibus) | [---]mae? maȋr[i?] | [---]M(a?)ximi et A (?) | ....MI|[---].

93. Fragment of the funerary slab of limestone height 47 width 35 thick 26 cm. Portrait of the deceased in the upper part. Discovered in 1966 'out of the south side of the tomb V'. Unpublished.

D(is) M(anibus) [s(acrum)] | Stre[....]| ,EA[

94. Fragment of the funerary slab of limestone, discovered in the necropolis II 1974, in the quadrant III, height 10.7, width 12, thick 25 cm. Letters 4 cm high.

SO[ ]
ET [ ]

V. PECULIARITIES OF THE NOMENCLATURE AND KINSHIP SYSTEM IN MUNICIPIUM S

a) NAMES WITH TWO COGNOMINA

Names, in some cases with praenomen and two cognomina appear often in the inscriptions in the region of Pljvlje and Prijepolje. This habit was characteristic of certain families, such as *Paconii* or *Titulli*. Both men and women bore two cognomina, in abbreviated forms or as full names. The next generation did not keep them or, if they did which happened very rarely, they were not the same as previously. The known samples, both in Pljevlje and Prijepolje are:

1. *Aur. Maximus Argenianus*, Aur.Maximina filia, no. **6**

2. *Aur. Titulla Arguriana* no. **46**

3. Her niece *Aurelia Titulla Cambria*

4. *T. Aur. Ru[f]us Belzeiu[s]* in the inscription found in Rosulje near Prijepolje, Spomenik 77, no. 17

5. His wife was *Aur. Fusca B[ ]*

6. *Statius Victor Brizidia*, no. **52**

7. *P. Ael.Pladome[nus] Carvanius* or *Carvanio*, Čadinje near Prijepolja, no. **1b**. His wife was *Aelia Panto*, his sons were Aelii Titus, Lupus and Firminus, no. **1b**

8. Aur. Severus Celsianus, no. **50**

9. *Paconia Montana R.*, no. **75**

10. Her mother *Aurelia Panto G.*

11. L.P(aconius) Barbarus d(ecuriio) m(unicipi) R. no. **5** The letter *R.* probably does not signify the name of the municipium, but belongs to the proper name

12. Titus PR.R., no. **56**

13. Luc[iu]s Valens Or. no. **83**.

Aplis Aureli Argurinus no. **48** have three names, but following an unusual nomenclature formula, with the native name as prename, the name Aurelius in the position of the patronymic and *Argurinus* as the cognomen.

In his paper *Die Namengebung der Urbevölkerung in der römischen Provinz Dalmatien*, BNF 15, 1964, 100, G. Alföldy quoted five samples of this kind from Pljevlja and Prijepolje which were known at that time: *T. Aur. Rufus Belzeius, P. Ael. Pladomenus Carvanius, Aur. Titulla Arguriana* and her niece *Aur. Titulla Cambria, Statius Victor Brizidia and T. Aur. Severus Celsianus* and explains them as having an onomastic form with two names which the Delmatae took over from the Liburni. He recognized the parallel formula in Liburnia in the name *L. Baebius Opiavi f. Ser. Oplus Malavicus*, CIL III 10121 or *Iulia C.f. Tertia Toruca*, CIL III 3015.[142] He explains the Romanized citizens' custom of having the old gentile name as cognomen as vestiges of the old system of nomenclature. Some of these names could have had a geographic meaning.

Alföldy seems to be right in suggesting that in these cases the vestiges of the old system of personal names are preserved. This explanation fits the form with the patronymic, such as *Cato Stataria Tu(r)i filia* which is known in Pljevlje and in the coastal zone of Dalmatia. However, it is not possible to find an explanation which could be applied to all samples, those in the region of the Delmatae on the one hand and in Plevlje and Prijepolje on the other. In contrast to the samples from western Dalmatia, in the inscriptions from Plevlje and Prijepolje filiation is lacking. Geographic meaning in some cases in Liburnia is possible as in the case of. *L. Baebius Opiavi f. Ser. Oplus Malavicus*, CIL III 10121, but it was not the case in the samples from the Lim and Ćehotina valley. The third name in inscription no. **2**, which differs for the aunt (*Arguriana*) and her niece (*Cambria*) could not be geographical in meaning. The second cognomen could have a different significance. It could have been added in order to separate families sharing the same *gentile*, but belonging to different families, as in the case of *Statii*: *Statius Victor Brizidia*, no. **52** has a third name, which proves that he did not belong together with *Statius Bessio*, in the inscription from Kolovrat or *Statia Fuscina*

---

[142] G. Alföldy, Bevölkerung, 62, n. 50, refering to D. Rendić-Miočević, Zbornik za historijske nauke u Zadru 1, 1955, 135.

in the inscription from Otilovići near Plevlje no. **40** or Statia *Am?[...]ena f. [.]isin*, no. **79** with the filiation. AM...ENAE, which could not be completed, may suggest the mother's name.

The third name might denote the cognatic kinship line. It could be applied to the mother's family as in the case of *Aurelia Titula Arguriana* and her niece *Aurelia Titula Cambria*, in the example 2 or in the family of *Paconii*. As the kinship was on the father's lineage (*amita*) both are *Titullae* which was the old gentile name which became the cognomen. The new gentile name *Aurelius* was added after the emperor who granted the family Roman *civitas*. The second cognomen, *Arguriana* in one name and *Cambria* in another could derive from the mother's gens which could not have been the same for the father's sister (*amita*) and her niece. The mother's *gens* could explain also the second cognomen in abbreviated form in the *Paconii* family. The third name is not the same in the name of the mother *Aurelia Panto G( )* and her daughter *Paconia Montana R( )*, on the one hand, but is the same in the name of the latter and Paconius Barbarus, probably her brother. The same *R( )* appears in the name of the city decurion *L. P(aconius) Barbarus d.m. R( )*, no. **5** who could have been the brother of *Paconia Montana R.* (no. **75**).

Two cognomina could represent the survival of the old social system in which the gens on the mother's line was one of the most important elements in the kinship relations.[143] In the process of Romanization many families accepted the name of the emperor who granted them *civitas* as their gentile name; the old name was kept as the cognomen. In some cases the geographic origin became more important than the kinship connection.

Families and kinship

The burials in necropolis II in Komini went on for one or two and exceptionally three generations. Both the monuments with inscriptions and the archaeological material belong to a relatively short period of time, from the first century to the end of the third or beginning of the fourth. Before and after that time the burials in necropolis II are few in number.[144] That means that the municipium in Komini lasted no longer than three centuries. *Paconii*, who had one tomb in the oldest part of the necropolis and another, which is estimated to belong the newest part of it probably lived in the municipium for two or three generations. In every single monument either one generation (husband and wife) or two (parents and children) appear. Grandparents and grandchildren appear in a few inscriptions. The families are seldom connected one to another. *Paconii* belonged to a large family group and were connected to *Cipii* and *Lurii*. As far as the names show, the rest of the people who are mentioned in the preserved inscriptions were not related to one another.

Inscriptions numbering more than two generations are few in the municipium. *avus/avia* and *nepos* seldom appear in the inscriptions from the municipium. *Avia* is attested once (no. **88**) in the case where the mother's lineage could be suggested, and *nepos* is mentioned in two inscriptions (no. **78, 87**). A large family of native origin which was Romanised partly in the second generation is illustrated by an inscription from Prijepolje:

M. Garašanin. Istorija Crne Gore 1967, 225-226; M. Mirković, Godišnjak CBI XIV, 1975, 99, no. 5 with photo.

D(is) M(anibus) s(acrum) | G( ) Sûricino | et Sêp(timiae) Când̂idâe | avis q(ui) v(ixit) an(nos) LXXV⁵| êt illa an(orum) LX | êt Âûn̂(elio) M̂aximo | d̂e(curioni) m(unicipii) q(ui) v̂(ixit) ân(nos) LV | êt Âûn̂(eliae) M̂adît̂âe q(uae) | v̂(ixit) a(nnos) XXXX par(entibus)¹⁰| êt Âûn̂(eliae) V̂enuco|ni soron̂ŝ q(uae) v̂(ixit) a(nnos) XVI | Âûn̂(elius) Lâvius d(ecurio) m(unicipii) | êt sibi v(ivus) p(osuit).

Line 2: *G(aio)*, line: 5 *ila,* line 8: *Madia*, line 9: XL, line: 10-11 *Aur(elia) Venu con(iugi) sorori*, line: 13 ET omisit, Garašanin.

The grandfather's name, *G. Suricinus,* bears an unusual form. The abbreviation G( ) probably denotes the old native gens which had to be adjusted to the Roman nomenclature with the gentile name. In the original native family one name was to be expected. The name *Aurelius* which appears in the next generation was acquired together with Roman *civitas* in the second half of the second century or at the beginning of the third. It represents only a status symbol. Everyone in this inscription, with the exception of the grandmother *Septimia Candida* and her son *Aurelius Maximus* who was a *decurio* in the municipium, have preserved their native name as cognomen: the grandfather is *Suricinus*, the mother is *Aurelia Madita*, and the sister *Aurelia Venuco*. Even the son in the third generation, who erected the monument, preserved the name Lavius as cognomen, which represents the Romanized form of the native *Lavo*. He was also *decurio municipii*, like his father.

b) MARRIAGE: NATIVES AND ROMANS

Marriages between Roman citizens and those bearing native names and gentile names *Aelius* and *Aurelius* or without them are common in the municipium. Children had common Roman names, such as Maximus, Maximilla and similar. Only one son, whose parents bear only one native name, without *gentile*, had a native name.

---

[143] The mother's lineage did not disappear even under the Romans, as some inscriptions in Dardania show (M. Mirković, Anthropology and epigraphy – the case of central Balkan region, Acta XII congressus intern. Epigr. Graecae et latinae, 2003, 965-972).
[144] Information by M. Ružić.

Table II

Wife	husband	children
Aelia Ursa	Ael. Bessus	
Apla	Aur[ ] Is[ ]	
Aur. Candida	Aur. Aper	
Aur. Panto	L.P(aconius) Barbar( )	Paconia Montana fil. Pac. Barb. fil.
Aur. Panto	Aurelius Quintus	
Panto	[...]AN ? Pant[ ]	
Panto	T. Aurel(io) Ingenuo	T. Aurel(ius) Maxi|[m]us
A]ure|[lia T]ata	Aure]lius [ ]	
Aurelia Testo	Sex. Statius Restitutus	
Aurelia Titto	Aur(elius) Carus	
Ti[tto?	Aur(elius) [ ]	Cami[a? f(ilia)
Aur(elia) Tritano	Aur(elius) Maxsimus	
Aur. Vendo	T. Aurel. Aplini	T. Aur. Turus
Aur. Vendo		Aur. Maximus
Aurel. Vendo	Aurelius Plarens	
Aur. Vendo	T. Aur. VS[ ]	
Vendo	Terens	Bessus
Aur. Fusca	T.Aur. Ru[f]us Belzeiu[s	
Catoni Statariae Tu(r)i	Q. Ael(ius) Statianus	
Clem[ ]	Iaro [.] RI	
Claudia Procula	Lucius Valens Or.	
Egnatia So[te]r[is]	P.Gavieno Candidiano	Gav[i]en[i]:Valerianus Candida Egnatius
Fl(avia) Marcella	Nantius Sexti	
Fusca Ana	Iarito Ar( )	
Lucida	Aur. Aper	
Martia	Herma	L. Ael. [.]entius
Paul(a) Gaudene	Titus PR.R.	
Maxillo ?	M. Ulp(ius) [..]us	
Ratonia Autumna	Asidonius Vitellianus, *centurio coh. I miliariae*	
Statia Am?[.]ena	Asclepiades	Statia Ser?[.]ensis
Aur. Turo		Pinsus
	T. Aur. Severus Celsianus	Aur. Plares
	T.Aelius Scae|vianus	Aelii: Titianus, Aelianus
	Aur. Maximus Argenianus	Aur. Masximina
Maximina	Pletor	Victorinus Statia Fusca

c) LATERAL KINSHIP: *AMITA*

Amita (the father's sister) *Aurelia Titulla Arguriana* appears in the inscription no. **46** together with her niece *Aurelia Titulla Cambria*. Their common name *Titulla* proves that they belonged to the same family. *Titulla* is a known name in Italy and in the provinces.[145] Here it is in the position of *cognomen*. Both also have the name *Aurelia*. In contrast to the aunt Arguriana, the niece is Cambria.

The term *amita* is seldom attested in the Roman inscriptions because the lateral kinship lost its importance in the classical époque when the nuclear family of father – mother – children prevailed. However the relationship *amita* and *fratris filia* (the father's sister and niece) retained its importance in classical times, even in juridical practice. As Gaius testifies, I 156,3,14, the niece could inherit the aunt on the father's line: *fratris filia legitima heres esse*.

The inscription of *Aurelia Titulla Arguriana* and *Aurelia Titulla Cambria* is important as one of the few testifying to the lateral kinship on the father's side. Both have two cognomina. Their common name *Titulla* could be their ancient gentile name. Celtic origin is suggested for the second names, *Arguriana* and *Cambria*. The element *Argu-* is recognized as Celtic (Holder I 214 and III 682 f.). The name *Cambria* could also be Celtic.[146] From it derived *Cambrianus* which appears in inscription no. **47** found in the surroundings of the municipium, in the present day village of Radosavac. Since *Titulla* represented the name in the father's line, *Arguriana* for *amita* and *Cambria* for her niece could derive from the mother's name in both cases.

A*mita* is also attested in Knin in the coastal zone in Dalmatia and again represents the common element in two regions.[147]

The father's sister – niece relationship is to be supposed once more, in another inscription from the muniicipium in the family linked with *Paconii*. Luria Frunita erected the funeral monument to her brother Cipius Faustus and his daughter Frunita *(fratri et nepti)* together with L. Paconius Barbarius who is named *cognatus*. no. **78**:

D(is) M(anibus) s(acrum) Cipio Fausto et Frunitae fil(iae) L. Paconius Barbario cognatus et Luria Frunita fratri et nepti.

The kinship relationship in this inscription is difficult to reconstruct for various reasons. Firstly, some names are missing, the name of Cipius's wife and the gentile name of the daughter Frunita; further, Cipius Faustus and his sister Luria Frunita have different gentile names. They must have had the same mother but probably not the same father. It is also unclear whose *cognatus* was Paconius Barbario from the the prominent municipal family *Paconii* attested in many inscriptions. He could have been related to the mother of Luria Frunita and Cipius Faustus or of his unnamed wife and the mother of Frunita, or even the husband of Luria Frunita. Assuming that the term *neptis* has the meaning of niece, and not granddaughter, which would be expected, the family links could be reconstructed as follows: if *frater* has the meaning of the biologic brother and a *neptis* signifies niece, Luria Frunita, the sister of Cipius Faustus erected the monument together with L. Paconius Barbario *cognatus* to her brother and her niece. Luria Frunita must be *amita*, i.e. the aunt on the father's line. Another possibility is to grant to the term *neptis* the usual meaning of granddaughter. That meant that Luria Frunita dedicated the monument to her brother and his daughter Frunita who was her granddaughter. In this case the marriage of the brother with his sister's daughter whose name is omitted could be suggested.

---

[145] Lörincz, Onomasticon, s.v.
[146] G. Alföldy, Bevölkerung, 56 i BN 15, 1964, 99.
[147] *Amita* appears in inscriptions from the coastal zone in Dalmatia, in Corinium, CIL III 2891. There is an incongruity in this inscription concerning mother's gentile name which is the same as that of her husband's sister, who is her daughter's *amita*. It is possible that the term *amita* was there in use instead of the *matertera*, which means the mother's sister.

CONCLUSION

The inscriptions and archaeological findings in the necropolises in Komini indicate that life in the municipium lasted no longer than two or three generations. A peculiarity of the city life is the presence of a large number of natives in the city community. As far as it is possible to conclude from the analysis of the names in the inscriptions, they belonged either to the pre-Roman stratum which was the same as in the large territory from the Adriatic coast to the river Drina or to the people who were transported by the Romans from the coastal zone and the region inhabited by the Delmatae in the inland of the province of Dalmatia. The presence of the pre-Roman population in the middle of the Balkans, between the Adriatic coast and the river Morava on the east, reveal common elements in the material culture in the until now discovered burials and cemeteries[148] and some of the Illyrian names which are known in the large zone of the so called middle Dalmatian region.

The indigenous population in the area of the Lim and Ćehotina valley probably survived until Roman times, but not in great numbers. Both onomastic and archaeological criteria reveal little about this stratum. Archaeological research reveals the problem of a several centuries-long gap between the early Iron Age and the Roman period in the area of Pljevlja and Prijepolje, as for instance the discoveries in Ljutići and Otilovići show. Close to the prehistoric early Iron Age tumuli are discovered the Roman gravestones. At the Radoinja cemetery near Nova Varoš there was a re-use of the prehistoric tumulus, into which late antique inhumations and cremations were inserted.[149] This could mean that this region was deserted during the early Iron Age for some unknown reasons and inhabited again in Roman times. However, if the name reflected the ethnic situation, natives did not disappear from this region even in the late second and the beginning of the third centuries. Names which could be attributed to the peoples living in the large area from the Adriatic coast and the region between the Krka and Cetina rivers inhabited by the Delmatae to the Morawa valley are preserved in the large number. The majority of names in the inscriptions from Pljevlja have close parallels with those in the Dalmatian region, especially in Rider and Vrlike. Only a few of them have parallels in the central region, far from the sea as for instance in Karan near Užice where the burial findings show a similarity with those from both necropolis at Komini. None of these names appear in the inscriptions from Kosovo. The large number of names in the inscriptions from Komini with parallels in the region inhabited by the Delmatae in the historical period speaks in favour of the hypothesis about the transportation from the territory of Delmatae to the region of Komini and Kolovrat. However, there are names which appear only in the inscriptions from Pljevlja and others which are known only from the inscriptions in Prijepolje. It could be suggested that part of the people in both settlements belonged to specific groups which differ from one another and from the rest of the inhabitants in the middle Dalmatian region. That could mean that the rest of the old population survived.

The large number of common names in the region inhabited by Delmatae and in the Roman settlements near Plevlje and in Prijepolje as well as the nomenclature formulae with two cognomina could be interpreted as one more element which points to the common origin of the people in the Lim and Ćehotina valley and Delmatae and the people in the coastal zone in Dalmatia. However the question as to whether they all belonged to the pre-Roman substratum in the middle Dalmatian zone from the Adriatic cost to the river Drina, or that the similarity of the onomastic in two regions so far apart is due to migration from the region of Delmatae to the region of Plevlje and Prijepolje under Roman rule remains without a definite answer.

In the inscriptions from the municipium and the surrounding countryside some people appear with sole, mostly native names and it is to assume that they retained

---

[148] Cf. synthesis by R. Zotović, Population and Economy of the Eastern Part of the Roman Province of Dalmatia, BAR Intern. Series 1010, Oxford 2002, resumed by J.J. Wilkes, Cultural identities in the Illyrian Provinces (2nd century BC 3th century AD: some old problems re-examined, Atti del convegno internazionale, Dall' Adriatico al Danubio. L' Illyrico nell'eta greca e romana, Cividale del Friuli, 25-27 settembre 2003, ed. G. Urso, Pisa 2004, 309-318).

[149] Zotovic, 40 ff.; Wilkes, 311.

their peregine status. The majority of people, however, appear with a Roman gentile name in the onomastics with two or three names. The native name is usually preserved in the position of cognomen.

The Roman nomenclature formula indicates in many cases a peculiarity of the social system which is common in the Roman settlements in Komini near Pljevlje and in Kolovrat in the vicinity of Prijepolje. A number of names appear with two cognomina which could signify the link with the old gens. To the peculiarities of the region belong the link with the father's lateral family, as was the father's sister *amita*. That could mean that the the extended family survived in the Roman municipium.

Inscriptions and the topography of the necropolis II do not reflect any social division between Romans and natives. Persons with native names appear together with Romans in the same families and in the same monuments.

ABBREVIATIONS

Acta ant. hung. = Acta antiqua Academiae scientiarum Hungaricae (Budapest)

Acta arch. hung. = Acta archaeologica Academiae scientiarum Hungaricae (Budapest)

AE = Année épigraphique

AEM = Archaeologisch-epigraphische Mitteilungen, Wien

Arch Jug. = Arcaeologia Iugoslavica, Beograd

Alföldy, PND = G. Alföldy, Die Personennamen der römischen Provinz Dalmatia, Heidelberg, 1969

Alföldy, Bevölkerung = Bevölkerung und Gesellschaft der römischen Provinz Dalmatien, Budapest, 1965

Alföldy, Nemengebung = G. Alföldy, Die Namengebung der Urbevölkerung in der römischen Provinz Dalmatia, Beiträge zur Namenforschung 15, 1964

BNF = Beiträge zur Namewnforchung

Bull-Dalm = Bulletino di archeologia e storia dalmata, Split

Evans, Antiquarian Researches = A.J. Evans, Antiquarian Researches in Illyricum, Archaeologia XLIX, London, 1885

Godišnjak CBI = Godišnjak Centra za Balkanološka istraživanja, Sarajevo

IDR = Inscriptiile Daciei Romane

Detschew, Thr. Sprach. = D. Detschew, Die Thrakische Sprachreste, Wien 1957

GZM = Godišnjak Zemaljskog muzeja Bosne i Hercegovine, Sarajevo

Holder, I-III = A. Holder, Altceltischer Sprachschatz I-III

ILJug = A. et J. Šašel, Inscriptiones quae in Jugoslavia inter annos ... et annos...repertae et editae sunt (Ljubljana)

IMS = Inscriptions de la Mései Supérieure (Beograd)

JÖAI = Jahreshefte des Österreichischen Archäologischen Instituts (Wien)

Katičić, MDN = R. Katičić, Das mitteldalmatische Namengebiet, Živa antika 12, 1963, 255-292

Katičić, SIN = R. Katičić, Die illyrischen Personennamen in ihrem südöstlichen Verbeitungsgebiet, Živa antika 12, 1962, 95-120

Lörincz, Onomasticon = Onomasticon provinciarum Europae latinarum I – IV, Budapest 2005

Mayer, Ill. Sprache = A. Mayer, Die Sprache der alten Illyrier, Wien 1957

D. Rendić-Miočević, Ilirska onomastika = Rendić-Miočević, D., Ilirska onomastika na latinskim natpisima Dalmacije

Sergejevski, Spomenik = D. Sergejevski, Rimski spomenici iz Bosne, Spomenik SKA XCVIII 1941

Spomenik SKA = Spomenik Srpske kraljevske akademije, Beograd

VHAD = Vjesnik Hrvatskog arheološkog društva, Zagreb

Vulić, Spomenik = N. Vulić, Antički spomenici naše zemlje, Spomenik SKA LXXI, 1933, LXXV, 1935, XCVIII, 1941-1948

Wilkes, Dalmatia = J.J. Wilkes, Dalmatia, History of the provinces of the Roman Empire, London, 1969

WMBH = Wissenschaftliche Mitteilungen aus Bosnien und Herzegovina

ZPE = Zeitschrft für Papyrologie and Epigraphik

BIBLIOGRAPHY

ALFÖLDY, G. – Bevölkerung und Gesellschaft der römischen Provinz Dalmatien, Budapest 1965.

ALFÖLDY, G. – Σπλαυνον – Splonum, Acta ant. hung. 10, 1-2, 1962, 3-12.

ALFÖLDY, G. – Die Namengebung der Urbevölkerung in der römischen Provinz Dalmatia, Beiträge zur Namenforschung 15, 1964, 98-102.

ALFÖLDY, G. – Die Personennamen der römischen Provinz Dalmatia, Heidelberg 1969.

ALFÖLDY, G. – Die Auxiliartruppen der Provinz Dalmatien, Mavors Roman Army Researches, III, 1987, 252.

BLAU, O., Monatsberichte der königlich preusischen Akademie der Wissenschaften zu Berlin, aus dem Jahr 1866, Berlin 1867, 638-854.

BOUÉ, Ami – *La Turqui de Europe*, Paris 1840.

CERMANOVIĆ-KUZMANOVIĆ, A. – Rezultati arheoloških istraživanja na poduručju Municipijuma S...kod Prijepolja – selo Komini, Kongres arheologa Jugoslavije Materijali IV, Herzeg Novi 1966, 77-83.

CERMANOVIĆ-KUZMANOVIĆ, A. – Neue Funde aus dem Municipium S., Hommages à Marcel Renard III, Collection Latomus vol. 103, 1969, 116-123, tf. XXXIX-XLII.

CERMANOVIĆ-KUZMANOVIĆ, A. – Novi epigrafski spomenici iz Komina I Kolovrata, Starinar 32, 1981, 75-79.

CERMANOVIĆ-KUZMANOVIĆ, A. – Nekoliko neobjavljenih natpisa iz Komina, Zbornik Filozofskog fakulteta u Beogradu XI-1, 1970, 75-81.

CERMANOVIĆ-KUZMANOVIĆ, A. – Die Porträts an den Grabdenkmälern aus Komini und Kolovrat, Balcanica 23, 1972, 441-446.

CERMANOVIĆ-KUZMANOVIĆ, A. – Die Römische-illyrischen Skulpturen aus Komini, Antike Welt 2, 1973, 6-7.

CERMANOVIĆ-KUZMANOVIĆ, A. – Rezultatai novih arheoloških istraživanja na području Municipijuma S. u selu Komini, Simpozijum "Seoski dani Sretena Vukosavljevića IV. 1976, 93-99.

CERMANOVIĆ-KUZMANOVIĆ, A. – Rimsko-ilirska plastika u Kominima, Živa antika 28, 1978, 325-330.

CERMANOVIĆ-KUZMANOVIĆ, A. – Rezultati arheoloških istraživanja u selu Komini (Municipium S...), Starine Crne Gore VI, Cetinje 1979, 93-99.

CERMANOVIĆ-KUZMANOVIĆ, A. – Rezultati arheoloških istraživanja u selu Komini (Municipium S...), Starine Crne Gore VI, Cetinje 1979, 93-99.

CERMANOVIĆ-KUZMANOVIĆ, A. – Vorrömische Elemente in der Kultur des Municipium S. im Dorfe Komini, Živa antika 30, 1980, 227-232.

CERMANOVIĆ-KUZMANOVIĆ, A. – Komini – Municipium S..., nekropole, Beograd 1998.

CERMANOVIĆ KUZMANOVIĆ, A., D. SREJOVIĆ, S. MARKOVIĆ – Necropoles romaines á Komini prés de Pljevlja (Municipium S...), Inventaria archaeologica 15, 1972.

DETSCHEW, D. – Die thrakischen Sprachreste, Wien 1957.

EVANS, A.J. – Antiquarian Researches in Illyricum, Archaeologia XLIX, 1885.

HOERNES, M. – Römische Alterthümer in Bosnien und der Herzegovina, AEM IV, 1880, 187-196.

HOLDER, A. – Alt-keltischer Sprachschatz, I-III, Leipzig 1894-1916.

JOSIFOVSKA B. – Scupi et la région de Kumanovo, IMS VI, Beograd 1982.

KATICIC, R. – Das mitteldalmatische Namengebiet, Živa antika 12/2, 1963, 255-292.

KATICIC R. – Die südillyrischen Personennamen in ihrem südöstlichen Verbreitungsgebiet, Živa antika 12/1, 196394-120.

KATICIC R. – Zur Frage der keltischen und pannonischen Namengebiete im römischen Dalmatien, Godišnjak CBI 1, 1965, 53-76.

KRAHE, H. – Lexicon altillyrischer Personennamen, Heidelberg 1929.

LAZIĆ, M. – Humka iz Bronzanog doba na lokalitetu Savin lakat kod Prijepolja, Arhaika (Beograd) 1, 2007, 109-127.

LINK S. – Konzepte der Privilegierung römischer Soldaten, Stuttgart 1989.

LOMA S. – Princeps i peregrini incolae u municipijumu S(plonistarum?), Živa Antika 52, 2002, 143-179.

MAYER, A. – Die Sprache der alten Illyrier, Wien 1957.

MIRKOVIĆ, M. – Iz istorije Polimlja u rimsko doba. Godišnjak CBI XIV, 12, 1975, 95-108.

MIRKOVIĆ, M. – Roman military diplomas, epistulae and papyrological evidence, Proceedings of the 20th Intern. Cong. of Papyrologists, Copenhagen 23-29, August 1992, 425-455.

MIRKOVIĆ, M. – Antropology and epigraphy – the case of central Balkan region, Acta XII congressus interno. Epigr. Graecae et latinae, 2003, 965-972.

MIRKOVIĆ, M. – Beneficiarii consularis in Sirmium, Chiron 24, 1994, 348-295.

MIRKOVIĆ, M. – Military Diplomas from Viminacium and the Settlement of auxiliary veterans: city or countryside? In Kaiser, Heer und Gesellschaft in der Römischen Kaiserzeit, Gedenkenschrift für Eric Birley, ed. G. Alföldy, B. Dobson, W. Eck, Stuttgart 2000, 365-375.

MIRKOVIĆ, M. – Married and settled, the origo, privileges and settlement of auxiliary soldier, in Militärdiplome, Die Forschungsbeiträge der Berner Gespräche von 2004, ed. A. Speidel und H. Lieb, Stuttgart 2007, 327-343.

PAPAZOGLU, F. – The Central Balkan Tribes in pre-Roman times, Triballi, Autariatae, Dardanians, Scordisci and Moesians, Amsterdam 1978.

PAPAZOGLU, F. – Sur quelques noms "thraces" en Illyrie, Godišnjak XII CBI, 10, 1974, 59-72.

PAPAZOGLU, F. – Le municipium Malvesatium et son Territoire, Živa Antika 7, 1957, 113-122.

PATSCH, C. – Archaologisch-epigraphische Untersuchungen zur Geschichte der romischen Provinz Delmatien WMBH 4, 1896, 276-296, 8, 1902, 115-121 and 12, 1912, 117-130.

PATSCH, C. – Sandjak novopazarski u rimsko doba, GZM 6, 1894, 466-488.

PATSCH, C. – Thrakische Spuren an der Adria, JÖAI 10, 1907, 169-174.

POUQUEVILLE, F.C.H.L. – Voyage dans la Grèce, comprenant la description ancienne et moderne de l'Epire, de l'Illyrie grecque, de la Macédoine Cisaxienne, d'une partie de la Triballie, de la Tessalie, de l'Acarnanie, de l'Etolie ancienne et Epictète, de la Locride Hesperienne, de la Doride, et du Peloponèse; avec des considerations sur l'archéologie, la numismatique, les moeurs, les arts, l'industrie et la commerce des habitations de ces province, I-IV, Paris 1820-1821.

RENDIĆ-MIOČEVIĆ, D. – Ilirska onomastika na latinskim natpisima Dalmacije (III. Prilog Vjesniku za arheologiju i historiju dalmatinsku, sv. LII), Split 1948.

RENDIĆ-MIOČEVIĆ, D. – Princeps municipii Riditarum, Iliri i antički svijet, Split 1989. 853-869.

RITTERLING, Legio, RE XII, 1924.

Le ROUX, P. – Peregrini incolae, ZPE 154, 2005, 261-266.

SHERWIN WHITE, A.O. – The Roman Citizenship^2, 1973.

SREJOVIĆ, D. – Grobnice Aurelije Maksimine i Pakonije Montane u Kominima (Municipium S.), Zbornik Narodnog muzeja 8, Beograd 1975, 177-187.

Von ENGEL – Geschichte der Fraystaates Ragusa, Wien 1807.

WILKES, J.J. – Dalmatia, History of the provinces of the Roman Empire, London 1969.

WILKES, J.J. – Cultural identities in the Illyrian Provinces (2nd century BC 3rd century AD> some old problems re-examined, Atti del convegno internazionale, Dall' Adriatico al Danubio. L' Illyrico nell'eta greca e romana, Cividale del Friuli, 25-27 settembre 2003, ed. G. Urso, Pisa 2004, 309-318.

WILKES, J.J. – Arthur Evans in the Balkans 1875-81, repr. from Bulletin 13 of the Institute of Archaeology, 1976, 25-56.

WILKES, J.J. – Σπλαυνον – Splonum again, Acta antiqua hung. 13, 1965, 11-124.

ZOTOVIĆ, M. – Arheološki i etnički problemi bronzanog i gvozdenog doba zapadne Srbije, Beograd 1985.

ZOTOVIĆ, R. – Population and Economy of the Eastern Part of the Roman Province of Dalmatia, BAR Intern. Series 1010, Oxford 2002.

ADDENDUM:
NATIVE NAMES IN THE SURROUNDINGS OF PLJEVLJA AND PRIJEPOLJE AND IN THE REGION OF IVANGRAD

Belzeius: Rosulje near Prijepolje

95. Funerary monument height 132 width 72 thick 52. The inscription in the frame on the front side; on the left lateral side represented Attis. Damaged both, the monument and the inscription Found in the village Rosulje near Prijepolje.

Sergejevski, Spomenik SKA 77, 1934, 17, no. 21, with photo of the lateral side (A. et J. Šašel, ILJug. 1731). Sergejevski reads:

D(is) M(anibus) S(acrum) | T. Aur(elius) Ru[fu]s | Belzeiu[s] | viv(u)s sibi | et Aur(eliae) Fusc[ae] | b[enemerenti?---] | [--- an(norum)] | XX [---] m[en(sium---] | r(arissimae) m(ulieri) dom[um] | aetern[am] | fecit po|suit o(ssa) v(obis) b(ene).

The name *Belzeius* in the three names nomenclature formula is only on this monument known. Mayer defines it as Illyrian, Alföldy connects it with the Celtic *Belsus*. Rendić, Arh. Jug. 2, 1965, 45 suggests that it was a kind of ethnical name similar to Mazaeius.

Madussa: **Toci** near Priboj

96. Funerary monument of marble height 80 width 50 thick 19 cm. In the upper part under two arches two busts, female on the left side with the scarf which covers the her head and shoulders in the way as it was usual on the many monuments in the central Balkans and male on the right side. It was immured in the church in the village Toci.

Vulić, Spomenik 31, 1931, no. 316 with photo (A. et J. Šašel, ILJug. 1736).

D(is) M(anibus) s(acrum) | Au(relia) Madus|sa Aur(elio) Ma|uritano | coniugi | p(ientissimo) qui vi(xit) | an(nis) XXVII.

Alföldy consider *Madussa* Celtic, from the root *Madu* attested in the river Drina valley quoting Holder, Altcelt. Sprachsch. II 370; Katičić, Zur Frage der keltischen und pannonischen Namengebiete im römsichen Dalmatien, Godišnjak CBI 1, 1965, 53-76 disagree; for him the name is Illyric. *Maduus* and other derivations from the root *madu-* in Spain would rather speak in favor of Alföldy's opinion.

Lavius: Seljani

97. Altar of limestone, height 43 width 36 thick 63 cm. It was found near the orthodox church in Seljani, later used as the altar in the church, in the time when Vulić saw it.

Patsch, GZM 6, 1896, 487, no. 49, with drawing fig. 34; idem WMBH 4, 1896, 291, no. 49 with drawing of the first three lines of the inscription (CIL III 13848); Vulić, Spomenik 71, 1931, no. 337 and idem, Spomenik 98, 1941-1948, no. 336 with the drawing by Sergejevski (A. et J. Šašel, ILJug. 1962).

I(ovi) O(ptimo) M(aximo) | C(o)hort(ali) | Aur(elius) La|vius ex | v(oto) l(ibens) p(osuit).

The name in the line 3 could be *Lautus*

Lavianus: Džurovo on the left Lim bank:

98. Altar noted by A. Deroko and I. Zdravković, Starinar 1, 1950, 183-184 (A. et J. Šašel, ILJug. 75A).

Herc(uli) Aug(usto) | sac(rum) Titus | Ael(ius) Lavia|nus II vir | et Cassius | Firmus v(otum) | l(ibens) m(erito) s(olverunt).

Pladomenus, Carvanio, Panto in the inscription no. **1b** found in **Čadinje** near Prijepolje.

Turo, -onis: Derikonjići:

99. Funerary monument of the marble height 150 width 105 thick 17 cm. In the upper part in the aedicule under three arches three portraits, two female with the scarf on

their heads arranged in the usual ways to cover shoulders. It was found in the village Derikonjići.

Vulić, Spomenik 71, 1931, no. 331 with photo (A. et J. Šašel, ILJug. 1696).

> *D(is) M(anibus) | Aurelia[e] | Turoni[---] | [--]vio | VEIT | heres | pos(uit).*

Line 3: *Tuboni* Vulić

Native names in the region of Ivangrad (Berani) to-day

This region was inhabited probably by the same people as the area between Pljevlja and Prijepolje. The name *Verzalio* in the inscription from **Budimlje** near Ivangrad has the parallel only in Komini near Pljevlja:

Budimlje: Verzalio

100. N Funerary monument of limestone height 110 width 60 cm; On the upper part three busts. It was immured in portal in the south wall of the church Djurdjevi Stupovi near Ivangrad. Transported probably from Budimlje in 1780 (Vulić).

CIL III 13832; Vulić, Spomenik 71, 1931, no. 11 with photo (A. et J. Šašel, ILJug. 1814).

> *D(is) Ma(nibus) s(acrum) | Aur(elio) Verzalio | liberto qu(i) | vuxsit (!) an|nis LXXXXV.*

Line 2: Verzaiio Vulić, Verzatio Šašel on the ground of photo.

Terent-: Lužac

101. Funerary slab of limestone height 180 width 55 thick 25 cm. In the upper part represented gable and aedicule with three portraits, two adults and one child between them. Found in the village Lužac in the house of the family Stojanović, later transported in the church Djurdjevi Stupovi in Ivangrad.

Vulić, Spomenik 71, 1931, no. 12 (A. et J. Šašel, ILJug. 1816).

> *D(is) M(anibus) S(acrum) | Teren|toni pa|tri pientis|simo qu(i) vix(it) an(nis) LV | L. Marcus | filius ei | et sib[i] vi|vus p(osuit)*

APPENDIX: INSCRIPTIONS

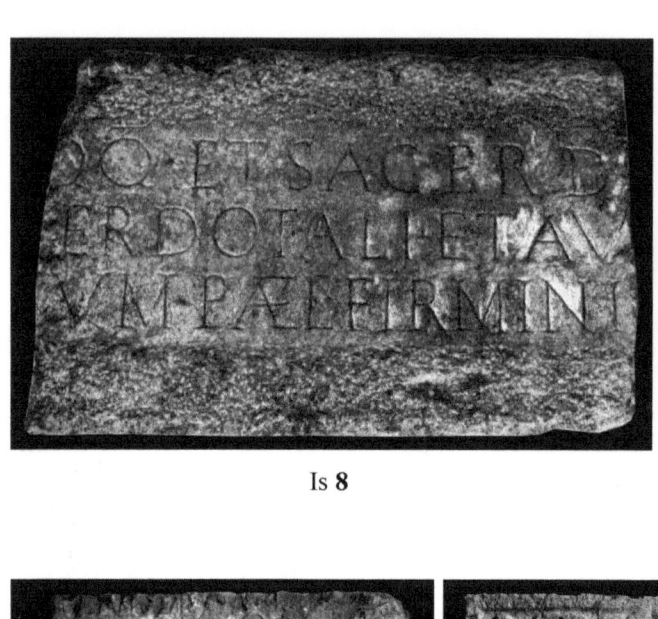

Is 8

Is 9

Is 11

Is 13

Is 14

APPENDIX: INSCRIPTIONS

Is 15

Is 16

Is 17

Is 35

Is 38

Is 39

Is 40

Is 41

Is 42

Is 43

Is 44

APPENDIX: INSCRIPTIONS

Is **45**

Is **46**

Is **47**

Is **48a**

Is **48b**

Is **49**

Is 50 Is 52 Is 54

Is 55 Is 56 Is 57

Appendix: Inscriptions

Is **58**

Is **59**

Is **60**

Is **61**

Is **62**

Is **64**

Is 70

Is 72

Is 73

Is 75a

Is 75b

Is 75c

Appendix: Inscriptions

Is 76

Is 77

Is 78

Is 79

Is 82

Is 83

Is 84

Is 86

Is 87

Is 88

Is 92

Is 93

Is 95

INDEX

Numbers in plain script refer to pages and numbers in bold script to inscriptions.

NOMINA VIRORUM ET MULIERUM
Aelia Panto 50, 61; **1b**
Aelia Ursa 46, 63; **33**
Aelius Aelianus **62**
Aelius Bessus 18, 46, 63; **33**
Q. Aelius [Fau]st[us] **80**
Aelius Felicianus 35; **35**
P. Aelius Firminus **8**
P. Aelius Fuscinus **12**
Titus Aelius Lavianus 48, 49; **98**
P. Aelius Pladomenus Carvanio 5, 42, 50, 61; **1b**
Aelius Quintus **23**
T. Aelius Scaevianus 63; **62**
Q. Aelius Statianus 63; **53**
Aelius Titianus 63; **62**
Aelius Tito 18; **55**
L. Aelius [- - -]ntius **32**
Aemilius Antoninus **71**
Aemilius Antoninus **71**
M. Aemilius Antonius 5, 38, 54; **3, 69, 70,**
Aemilius Calvinus **71**
M. Aemilius Titianus 38, **4**
Asidonius Vitellianus 63; **15**
Aurelia Candida 63; **30**
Aurelia Fusca 44, 61, 63; **95**
Aurelia Madita 18, 48, 62
Aurelia Madussa **96**
Aurelia Maximina 45, 61, 63; **6**
Aurelia Panto 17, 49, 55, 61, 62, 63; **5, 37, 59, 75**
Aurelia Tata 63; **63**
Aurelia Testo 18, 19, 58, 63; **22**
Aurelia Titto 63; **24**
Aurelia Titulla Arguriana 17, 54, 61, 62, 64; **46**
Aurelia Titulla Cambria 17, 54, 61, 62, 64; **46**
Aurelia Tritano 50, 63; **26**
Aurelia Turo 47, 63; **51, 99**
Aurelia Vendo 18, 19, 46, 47, 63; **16, 17, 27, 49**
Aurelia Venuco 48, 62

Aurelia [- - -]to **37**
Aurelius 54; **48**
T. Aurelius **16**
Aurelius Aper 63; **29, 30**
Sex. Aurelius Arg( ) 6, 54; **45**
Aurelius Carus 63; **24**
T. Aurelius Ingenuus 63; **60**
Aurelius Lavius 18, 62; **55, 97**
T. Aurelius Lupercus **1**
Sex. Aurelius Lupianus **42**
Aurelius Mauritanus **96**
Aurelius Maximus 45, 46, 62, 63; **17, 26**
T. Aurelius Maximus 63; **60**
Aurelius Maximus Argenianus 8, 17, 31, 54, 61, 63; **6**
Aurelius Plares 17, 63; **50**
Aurelius Plarens 17, 63; **49**
T. Aurelius Quintus 63; **59**
Aurelius Ru[fus] **81**
T. Aurelius Rufus Belzeius 44, 61, 63; **95**
T. Aurelius Severus Celsianus 6, 61, 63; **50**
T. Aurelius Sextianus 4; **1**
[A]urelius Ti[- - -] **91**
T. Aurelius Turus 18, 46, 47, 63; **16**
Aurelius Verzalius **100**
T. Aurelius VS[- - -] 46, 63; **27**
Aurelius [- - -] 63; **8, 25, 63**
Aur( ) **31**
T. Au[r( )] **90**
Aur( ) Is[- - -] 63; **14**
Sex. Baberius Ianuarius **82**
Caesia Asteris **72**
Cassius Firmus **98**
L. Cipius Faustus 64; **78**
Claudia Procula 63; **83**
Cornificius Verus **84**
Egnatia Soteris 63; **73**
C. Egnatius Montanus **72**
Flavia Marcella 63; **58**
Flavius Aper 8; **13**
Flavius Saturninus **11**
M. Fulvinus Natalis **87**

83

G( ) Suricinus 62
Aulus Gabilius Liberalis **13**
Gaviena Candida 63; **73**
P. Gavienus Candidianus 63; **73**
Gavienus Egnatius 63; **73**
Gavienus Valerianus 63; **73**
Gavius Durus **54**
Lucius Valens Or( ) 61, 63; **83**
Luria Frunita 64; **78**
Paconia Montana 8, 49, 55, 61, 62, 63; **75**
L. Paconius Barbario 49, 57, 64; **76, 77, 78**
L. Paconius Barbarus 8, 31, 49, 55, 61, 62, 63; **5**
L. Paconius Barbar( ) 49, 55, 63; **5**
M. Pl( ) Ursinus **77**
Ratonia Autumna 63; **15**
Septimia Candida 48, 62
Septimia Ov[i]n[. . .]ina **88**
Statia Am[.]ena 19, 62, 63; **79**
Statia Fuscina 44, 58, 61; **40**
Statia Lavo 18, 48, 58
Statia Ser[.]ensis 63; **79**
Statius Bessio 19, 46, 58, 61
Sex. Statius Restitutus 19, 58, 63; **22**
Statius Velocianus 58
Statius Victor Brizidia 17, 19, 58, 61; **52**
M. Ulpius Gellianus **2**
M. Ulpius [- - -]us 63; **57**
Valeria Te[sto ?] **23**
L. Valerius Celer **86**
Valerius Faustus 57; **76**
Valerius Optatus 48, 58
Q. Valerius Quadratus **86**
[- - -]ius St[- - -]ius **7**

COGNOMINA VIRORUM ET MULIERUM
Ae( ) **45**
Aelianus 63; **62**
Amabilis **85**
Am?[.]ena 19, 63; **79**
Ana 17, 18, 20, 40, 41, 44, 46, 48, 49, 63; **43**
Anna 58
Antoninus **71**
Antonius 5, 38; **3, 69, 70, 71**
Aper 8, 18, 63; **13, 29, 30**
Apla 17, 19, 20, 21, 35, 46, 63; **14**
Aplis 17, 18, 19, 20, 21, 36, 46, 47, 48, 50, 54, 61, 63; **16, 48**
Ar( ) **43**
Argenianus 8, 17, 20, 22, 31, 44, 45, 54, 61, 63; **6**
Arguriana 17, 45, 54, 61, 62, 64; **46**
Argurinus 21, 45, 46, 54, 61; **48**
Arg( ) 6, 54; **45**
Arvus 45, 63
Ar( ) **43**
Asclepiades 55, 63; **79**
Asteris **72**
Aula **87**

Autumna 63; **15**
Barbario 49, 64; **76, 77, 78**
Barbarus 8, 31, 49, 55, 61, 62, 63; **5**
Barbar( ) 55, 63; **5**
Belzeius 18, 20, 21, 22, 44, 61, 63, 71; **95**
Bessio 18, 19, 22, 46, 58, 61
Bessus 17, 18, 20, 22, 39, 46, 58, 63; **28, 33**
Brizidia 17, 19, 20, 22, 47, 58, 61; **52**
Calvinus **71**
Cambria 17, 20, 22, 45, 54, 61, 62, 64; **46**
Cambrianus 4, 17, 20, 45, 50, 54, 64; **47**
Camia 50, 63; **25**
Candida 48, 62, 63; **30, 73**
Candidianus 63; **73**
Carus 63; **24**
Carvanio 5, 18, 20, 22, 29, 50, 61, 71; **1b**
Cato 17, 18, 19, 20, 21, 47, 61; **53**
Celer **86**
Celsianus 6, 61, 63; **50**
Cep[ius] **88**
Certus **87**
Clem[- - -] 63; **44**
Despotianus **88**
Dexter **85**
Durus 17, 20, 22, 48, 55; **54**
Egnatius 63; **73**
Faustus 57, 64; **76, 78**
[Fau]st[us ?] **80**
Felicianius 35; **35**
Fiaetia 35; **35**
Firminus 61; **1b, 8**
Firmus **98**
Frunita 64; **78**
Fusca 17, 40, 41, 44, 58, 61, 63; **34, 43, 95**
Fuscina 41, 44, 58, 61; **40**
Fuscinus **12**
Gaudene 48, 49, 63; **56**
Gellianus **2**
Germanus 18, 19, 20, 22, 38, 48; **20**
Herma 63; **32**
Ianuarius **38, 82**
Iarito 20, 22, 63; **43**
Iaro 17, 44, 63; **44**
Ingenuus 63; **60**
Is[- - -] **14**
Lavianus 18, 48, 49; **98**
Lavius 17, 18, 19, 20, 21, 47, 48, 51, 62; **55, 97**
Lavo 18, 20, 48, 58
Liberalis **13**
Lucida 63; **29**
Lupercus **1**
Lupianus **42**
Lupus 61; **1b, 42**
Madita 18, 20, 22, 48, 62
Madussa 18, 21, 71; **96**
Marcella 63; **58**
Marcus **101**

Martia 63; **32**
Mauritanus **96**
Maxillo 17, 20, 22, 49, 52, 63; **57**
Maxima **87**
Maximilla **85**
Maximina 45, 58, 61, 63; **6, 40**
Maximus 17, 31, 35, 45, 46, 48, 54, 61, 62, 63; **6, 17, 26, 35, 39, 60, 92**
Montana 8, 49, 55, 61, 62, 63; **75**
Montanus **73**
Nantius 17, 20, 49, 63; **58**
Natalis **87**
Ni[- - -] **20**
Optatus 48, 58
Or( ) 61, 63; **83**
Ov[i]n[. . .]ina **88**
Pant[- - -] 63; **61**
Panto 17, 18, 19, 20, 21, 38, 41, 47, 49, 50, 55, 57, 61, 62, 63, 71; **1b, 5, 37, 59, 60, 61, 75**
[Pan]to **21**
Paris **74**
Paula 48, 49, 63; **56**
Pinsus 17, 18, 19, 20, 21, 22, 47, 63; **51**
Pladomenus 5, 18, 19, 20, 21, 28, 29, 50, 71; **1b**
Plares 17, 18, 19, 20, 22, 47, 63; **50**
Plarens 17, 22, 47, 63; **49**
Pletor 17, 20, 41, 50, 58, 63; **40**
Procula 63; **83**
P[.]a 58
Quadratus **86**
Quintus 63; **23, 59**
Restitutus 19, 58, 63; **22**
Rufinus **39**
Rufus 44, 61, 63; **95**
Ru[fus] **81**
R( ) **88**
Sabinus **87**
Saturninus **11**
Scaevianus 17, 20, 22, 50, 63; **62**
Ser[.]ensis 63; **79**
Severina 18, 44, 46, 58
Severus 6, 61; **50**
Sextianus 4; **1**
Sextus 63; **58**
Soteris 63; **73**
Stataria 20, 47, 48, 61, 63; **53**
Statianus 48, 63; **53**
Stre[- - -] **93**
St[- - -]ius **7**
Super **21**
Sv[- - -] **81**
Tata 17, 20, 50, 63; **64**
[T]ata **63**
Terens 17, 22, 39, 46, 63; **28**
Terentoni 18; **101**
Testo 18, 19, 20, 22, 38, 50, 58, 63; **22**
Te[sto] **23**

Titianus 38, 50, 63; **4, 62**
Tito 18, 20, 50; **55**
Titto 19, 20, 38, 50, 63; **24**
Ti[tto] **25**
Titulla 17, 45, 54, 61, 62, 64; **46**
Titus 17, 18, 44, 48, 49, 61, 63; **1b, 56**
Ti[- - -] **91**
Tritano 18, 19, 20, 50, 63; **26**
Turo 18, 19, 20, 47, 48, 63; **51, 99**
Turus 18, 19, 20, 22, 29, 36, 46, 47, 48, 49, 61, 63; **16, 53**
Ursa 46, 63; **33**
Ursina **77**
Ursinus **77**
U[.]sinu[- - -] **81**
Valens 61, 63; **83**
Valerianus 63; **54, 73**
Velocianus 58
Vendo 17, 18, 19, 20, 21, 29, 36, 39, 46, 47, 63; **16, 17, 27, 28, 49**
Venuco 18, 20, 48, 62
Verus **84**
Verzalius 18, 22, 51, 52; **100**
Verz[- - -] **65, 68**
Victor 17, 19, 58, 61; **52**
Victorinus 63; **40**
Vitellianus 63; **15**
VS[- - -] 63; **27**
[- - -]entius 63; **62**
[- - -]ma **92**
[- - -]to **37**
[- - -]unis **76**
[- - -]us 63; **38**
[- - -]vio **99**
[- - -]vunxus **21**

DII DEAEQUE
Genius municipii 30; **11**
Hercules Augustus **98**
Hercules, sanctus **84**
Isis **2**
Iuppiter Cohortalis 54; **69**
Iuppiter Optimus Maximus 54; **4, 12, 52**
Iuppiter Optimus Maximus Adventus **19**
Iuppiter Optimus Maximus Fulgurator 5, 54; **3**
Iuppiter Optimus Maximus Cohortalis **55, 97**
Nemesis, dea sancta 30; **11**
Serapis **2**
Silvanus Augustus 5, 54; **36, 70**
Sol Invictus **82**

RES SACRA
sacerdos **8**
sacerdotalis **8**

GEOGRAPHICA
Arbenses **2**
Maluensates **2**

Metlenses **2**
Municipium Aurelium S[p]lon(istarum) 5; **1b**
Municipium S( ) 4, 17; **1**
Risinium **79**
Salonae **71**
Scard( ) **15**
Splonistae **2**

IMPERATORES ET DOMUS EORUM
L. Aelius Aurelius Commodus Imperatoris T. Aelii Caesaris patris Antonini Augusti filius divi Hadriani nepos **10**
M. Opellius Antoninus Diadumenianus nobilissimus Caesar princeps iuventutis Caesaris M. Opellii Severi Macrini Pii Felicis Augusti filius **18**
C. Iulius Verus Maximinus Pius Felix et C. Iulius Verus Maximus nobilissimus Caesar **41**
Imperatores Augusti (duo) **19**

CONSULES
Imperatore L. Septimio Severo Pertinace Augusto et Albino Caesare consulibus (194) **12**

HONORES PUBLICI ROMANI
curator Arbensium Metlensium Splonistarum Maluensatium **2**
eques Romanus **1, 2**
praefectus civitatium [- - -]M 29, 42; **1b**

RES MILITARIS
Legiones
legio I Adiutrix **12**
legio XI Claudia **11**
legio XIII Gemina **35**

Auxilia
cohors II milliaria **15**

Munera militaria
beneficiarius **14**
beneficiarius consularis 11, 12, **13**
centurio **15**
miles 12, 17, **35**
veteranus **16**

RES MUNICIPALIS
decurio municipii 48, 54, 55, 61, 62; **5, 6, 7**
decurio municipii Aurelium S[p]lon(istarum) **1b**
decurio municipii S( ) 4; **1**
decuriones **42**
duovir **3, 98**
duovir quinquennalis 54; **4**
praefectus **1b**
princeps **42**
quinquennalis **8**

NOTABILIA VARIA
amita **46**
collega **42**
locus datus decreto decurionum **1, 9, 42**
pecunia publica decreto decurionum **18**
peregrini incolae **42**
populares **42**
populus **19**

NOMINA LOCORUM RECENTIORUM
Babiš Potok **52**
Budimlje **100**
Čadinje **1b**
Derikonjići **99**
Džurovo **98**
Gradac **39**
Ilijino Brdo **4, 18, 19, 20, 21, 22, 23, 24, 25, 26, 27, 28, 29, 30, 31, 32, 33, 34, 35**
Komini **5, 6, 7, 11, 13, 14, 15, 16, 17, 44, 47, 49, 50, 51, 54, 55, 56, 57, 58, 60, 61, 64, 65, 66, 67, 68, 74, 75, 79, 80, 82, 83, 84, 86, 87, 90, 91, 92, 93**
Lužac **101**
Ljutić **38**
Otilovići **40, 41**
Pljevlja **1, 3, 8, 9, 10, 12, 31, 42, 43, 45, 46, 53, 59, 62, 63, 65, 69, 70, 71, 72, 76, 77, 81, 85**
Podpeć **37**
Radosavac **36**
Rosulje **95**
Seljani **97**
Toci **96**

www.ingramcontent.com/pod-product-compliance
Lightning Source LLC
Chambersburg PA
CBHW061546010526
44113CB00023B/2814